AMERICA-
BRAINWASHED!

GIVING OUR COUNTRY AWAY

Billie Gorham

July 4, 2020

"All it takes for evil to prevail is for good men to do nothing."
Edmund Burke

The American people will never knowingly adopt Socialism, but under the name of "liberalism," they will adopt every fragment of the Socialist program until one day America will be a Socialist nation without knowing it happened. **—Norman Thomas,** American Socialist Party's presidential candidate, **1948**

President Ronald Reagan said,

"Freedom is never more than one generation away from extinction. It must be fought for, protected, and handed on for them (our children,) to do the same."

AMERICA BRAINWASHED!
Giving Our Country Away

©2020 Billie Gorham

print ISBN: 978-1-09832-328-8

CONTENTS

I HEAR AMERICA DYING!

Do you hear it? If you stop and listen, you can hear the tearing sound, the sound of a heart being sucked out, like the millions of babies being sucked out of a mother's womb - mothers who sacrificed their own babies on the altar of sex and selfishness.

But, it is America, my beloved America whose heart is being completely destroyed. It has become a nation of Nazis, a country of communists, a society of socialists, rewarding prostitutes, pedophiles and purveyors of pornography with freedom while punishing people who pray.

Where is the soul of the people? Where is America, land of the free, home of the brave? It has become the land of the liberals, and home of the homosexuals.

The government of the people, by the people and for the people is no more. It is a people NOT controlling their government but being controlled by it. It is a government that gradually took over our lives, promising free lunches if we would give up more of our freedoms. Suddenly, now, we have a government which is not even pretending to listen to the people. They took over the educational system a long time ago but have gradually taken control of the banking industry, the auto industry, the justice department, and now they are taking over the health care industry and the energy industry.

Ask yourself what is left? Agriculture? They only have to withdraw the farm subsidies to eliminate almost all of the farmers. Small businesses? The insurance, social security, employment taxes already make it impossible to make a profit and the large businesses have already moved overseas where the taxes and salaries are cheaper and where there are fewer government restrictions.

If you and I don't get on our knees and pray, then stand up and stop this greedy, power-hungry government, we will soon find ourselves dead in the ashes of a 200 year old experiment, successful beyond our wildest dreams, but destroyed by the degradation of our ugliest nightmares.

America! America! Is there any life left in you? Can you be healed? Can you rise up one more time to goodness and greatness?

Karl Marx, the founder of Communism, said, "My objective in life is to dethrone God and destroy capitalism."

America is forgetting what it means to be America.

Chapter 1
WE WILL CONQUER YOU!

The end of war is the control of a conquered people. If a people can be conquered in the absence of war, the end of war will have been achieved without the destruction of war. A worthy goal…and the glory of Commmunist conquest over the stupidity of the enemies of the People.

You are not alone if you are asking yourself, "What has happened to America?" Instead of a country founded on religious principals, we have a country that is openly hostile to those values. We live in a country that has made laws against virtue and for paganism, where government of the people, by the people and for the people has become a government that insists the people are wrong and must be over-ruled. Our country is now controlled by the most extreme liberals, determined to destroy our families, our children, our schools, our courts, our nation.

In this book, I will open up the background of what has been done and who is behind it. You will see that when you kept thinking about a conspiracy, you were right. It is indeed a conspiracy being implemented by those in the know and those who do not know. I am quoting the people themselves, using the very words of those who have been working against America so that you do not think it is my interpretation of what is happening, but will recognize the people and the plot behind it all.

The Bible warns, "My people perish for lack of knowledge," and indeed, we, through willful ignorance, have abandoned our country to those who have been plotting against it for generations.

We still have freedom-loving patriots. We still have heroes who have fought for freedom, who risk their lives to save others, who give generously to help the poor, to rescue their neighbors, who fight the bad guys. But our own government has been undermining our freedoms and our Constitution.

As we examine the people that we have positioned to protect and defend this country, I have been asking myself, "How did we get to the place that our civil servants would become our dictators? How did we get Congressmen and women who have been in office so long that they care nothing for America or its Constitution but are so attached to the power, influence, and money of the job that they are willing to commit any kind of corruption, compromise or deceit to ensure their position?"

As I looked at the people who were vying for the Democratic nomination, I asked, "What has become of common sense? These people are completely deluded in thinking that you can continually support everyone in the world with everything that they want. Free housing, free food, free healthcare, free education, free college, even free cell phones are being given to those who are willing to let the government take care of them.

These far-left Democrats are tickling the ears of the uneducated, the hopeless, the homeless, and the indolent who don't care about pride and responsibility but simply want what they want no matter who pays the bills and because they have been reared with that assumption, they believe they are entitled to it. It is called socialism and it may sound good unless you realize that someone has to pay. The thing about Socialists is that they believe everyone will be better off, but especially them. They believe that the masses can be herded and that they will get to do the herding. They think most of us are the unwashed "deplorables" and that they are the intelligentsia and know what is best for us and that they will still enjoy their luxury, power and prestige even though everyone else will lose everything.

Socialism may sound like a fine philosophy if you want to give away your freedom or if you believe that you will be one of the ones on top. It will end in a dictatorship and the destruction of the American way of life, liberty and the pursuit of happiness. If you don't believe that, look back at Russia. Look at Cuba, Venezuela. Look at what is happening in Hong Kong. Look at what the Chinese government has done and is doing to control every person in China.

I well remember the words Nikita Kruschev said when he visited America in the late 50's. He said, "We will take America without firing a shot...we will bury you."

As I write this, America is going through riots, burning, killing, destruction all over the country, something I thought I would never see. But we have an unfair justice system, not as much according to skin color as according to power and privilege which is subordinating justice to a lower rung of our republic. The ordinary citizen is angry because the people who are rich and powerful are getting by with breaking laws.

"Denying a Capitalist country easy access to courts, bringing about and supporting propaganda to destroy the home, creating continuous juvenile delinquency, forcing upon the state all manner of practices to divorce the child from it will in the end create the chaos necessary to Communism."

But it goes beyond socialism or communism. It is a conspiracy that has been manipulating us for centuries, using the same playbook that Communist governments and secret societies around the world have always used to take over countries. They intend to take over the world. First they have to get America out of the way.

Chapter 2
WE HAVE A PLAN!

"We can't expect the American people to jump from capitalism to communism, but we can assist their elected leaders in giving them small doses of socialism, until they awaken one day to find that they have communism." "We do not have to invade the United States; we will destroy you from within."

Kenneth Goff was a former card-carrying Communist from Englewood, Colorado. After seeing with alarm what was happening to America, he voluntarily appeared before the Un-American Activities Committee with THE RUSSIAN TEXTBOOK ON PSYCHO-POLITICS and this advice,

"This manual of the Communist Party should be in the hands of every loyal American, that they may be alerted to the fact that it is not always by armies and guns that a nation is conquered."

The quotes at the beginning of each chapter or those inserted that aren't referenced are from the book Kenneth Goff showed the committee that day and which was evidently disregarded. It is based on THE COMMUNIST MANIFESTO which was created by Karl Marx and Friedrich Engels and is a manual of how to take control of a government. When you can put the economy of a country in the hands of a few people, you will have power over the people. That is why some of our government leaders are promoting socialism. It isn't a share-the-wealth idea, as they want us to think. It is the rule that says, "Control-the-wealth and you can control the citizens."

Jan Kozak, wrote in the book, NOT A SHOT IS FIRED,

Communism is a tactic employed for the assumption of power, rather than a sincere belief. Americans who labor under the false premise that communism is either an ideology or a system of economics that died with the Cold War do so at their personal and national peril......There is no concern for the lot of the poor, or the conditions of the laborer, or even the wealth of the industrialist........power is the one and only goal."

Antonio Gramsci, an Italian Communist, concluded that in order to capture the power in a state, one must first capture the culture.

> "Belief in God, family, and limited government in the developed nations of the West constitutes a cultural system of 'fortresses and earthworks' against revolution."

That is why the primary goals for the take-over of America is to destroy the very foundations on which our system was built: faith, family and freedom.

Working to destroy the most conservative resistors first, the shadow government has made a full-fledged assault on religion, taking prayer out of schools, the Ten Commandments out of courthouses, legalizing abortion and accepting homosexuality. To destroy families and youth, the government is trying to obliterate the middle class by reducing their ability to provide for their families. Joseph Stalin recognized farmers to be his chief obstacle in controlling Russia and specifically Ukraine, "the bread-basket" of the Soviet Union, and that is why he starved millions of them to death.

The Communists also use the strategy of combining pressure from above with pressure from below to create policies to give the government more power. For example as the state was passing gun control laws throughout Eastern Europe, the Communist Party armed itself and took control of the police forces in those countries. That made it easy to take away freedom.

Our Second Amendment right to keep and bear arms is a defense against outlaws but also a protection against an outlaw government. That is why the Democratic Party is encouraging the demand for stricter gun laws every time there is a shooting in the U.S. They are combining their pressure from above with the pressure of the uninformed citizens and uneducated students below to create an atmosphere of conflict between those who see guns as the threat and those who see government as the threat.

Chapter 3
WE WILL DISTORT MAN'S VIEW OF HIMSELF!

"The first thing to be degraded in any nation is the state of Man, himself. Nations which have high ethical tone are difficult to conquer…. He must think of himself as an animal, capable only of animalistic reactions."

It was 1925, the ACLU advertised for a teacher who would be willing to challenge Tennessee's Butler Act, which prohibited teaching the theory of evolution in state public schools and universities. The law made it a misdemeanor punishable by a fine to "teach any theory that denies the story of the Divine Creation of man, and to teach instead that man has descended from a lower order of animals."

The so-called "Monkey Trial," in Dayton, Tennessee, began with John Thomas Scopes, a young high school science teacher, conspiring with a local businessman, George Rappalyea, to get charged with this violation. They were assisted by a famous attorney, Clarence Darrow. Hearing of this coordinated attack on Christian fundamentalism, William Jennings Bryan, the three-time Democratic presidential candidate and a fundamentalist hero, volunteered to assist the prosecution.

In front of several thousand spectators in the open air, Darrow called as his sole witness, Bryan, in an attempt to ridicule his literal interpretation of the Bible. Darrow forced Bryan to make contradictory statements to the amusement of the crowd, and then, in his closing speech, Darrow asked the jury to return a verdict of guilty in order that the case might be appealed, making it impossible for Bryan to deliver the closing speech he had been preparing for weeks. After eight minutes of deliberation, the jury returned with a guilty verdict, and Raulston ordered Scopes to pay a fine of $100.

Although Bryan had won the case, he had been publicly humiliated and his fundamentalist beliefs had been disgraced. Most people believe that Darrow and Evolution won that case. The reverse is true. As recently as 1930, an estimated 70% of all public high schools omitted all reference to the theory of evolution in their science classes. This situation prevailed for over three decades after the Scopes Trial. But, believing the lie that evolution won, we have allowed our schools to teach our children that they come from lower forms of animals. It was evident that the agenda of Darrow and the ACLU was not primarily to defend Scopes but to publicly discredit traditional religious beliefs.

By 1968, the Court held in Epperson vs. Arkansas that the prohibitions against teaching evolution were motivated by religious beliefs and therefore violated the First Amendment. Now, it is the opposite of what was taught in our schools for almost two hundred years. Now, you cannot teach creationism but are only allowed to teach the THEORY of evolution, the theory that completely contradicts the Bible which says that we were made in the image of God. How can our children attempt to be the best they can be, to "reach for the stars," when they have been taught they are nothing but animals?

Chapter 4
WE WILL DESTROY THE CHURCH!

"As it seems in foreign nations that the church is the most ennobling influence, each and every branch and activity of each and every church, must, one way or another, be discredited. Religion must become unfashionable by demonstrating broadly, through psychopolitical indoctrination, that the soul is non-existent, and that Man is an animal. Religion must be made synonymous with neurosis and psychosis."

Alexis de Tocqueville, a French political thinker and historian traveled this young country and wrote a book entitled, Democracy in America. Trying to discover what made America different from every other country, he said,

"I sought for the greatness and genius of America in her commodious harbors and her ample rivers-and it was not there ... in her fertile fields and boundless forests-and it was not there ...in her rich mines and her vast world commerce-and it was not there . . in her democratic Congress and her matchless Constitution-and it was not there. Not until I went into the churches of America and heard her pulpits flame with righteousness did I understand the secret of her genius and power. America is great because she is good, and if America ever ceases to be good, America will cease to be great."

Stalin, one of the most brutal dictators of all time, said,

"If we (the Communists) can destroy America's religion and morality, that is a key to undermining their culture and society. Then America will crumble from within."

Under the guise of defending our freedom, the American Civil Liberties Union, which is not American and was organized with the pretense of defending your liberties but in reality is eroding them, is busy transforming America. It has a plan and an ultimate goal:

"We have battled in America since the century's turn to bring to nothing any and all Christian influences and we are succeeding. While we today seem to be kind to the

10

Christian, remember we have yet to influence the 'Christian world' to our ends. When that is done we shall have an end of them everywhere."

The ACLU, the Socialists, the Communists and the Muslims all have as a goal to take over America. Once America as a free nation is destroyed, they can continue their agenda of a One World Government. To get there they must stop all things Christian, close the churches and reduce Christianity to "a crutch of the weak and helpless."

The ACLU incorporates in their agenda policies that will contribute to the church becoming less and less effective and noticeable.

Of course, the first thing that they did was to anchor the false theory of evolution to our classrooms and the next was to remove prayer and Bible readings from the schools so that children, especially those without Christianity in their homes, would have no foundation of truth on which to base their lives. People began to be afraid to pray.

Just two examples out of hundreds: In Tangipahoa Parish, Louisiana, attorneys with the ACLU demanded jail time for any person who prayed in a manner they disapproved of. In South Carolina and Virginia, the ACLU used the threat of a lawsuit against local government entities to silence prayer "in Jesus name.

If you could read the Policy Book of the ACLU, you would see what their real aims are. For instance, Policy No. 81 of the ACLU's agenda calls for a permanent ban on displays of the nativity scene and the menorah on public property, Policy No 84 calls for the removal of "under God" from the Pledge of Allegiance and "the Republic for which it stands," and Policy No 92 calls for an end to tax exemptions for all churches and synagogues.

They made steps toward that in 1954, when then-Sen. Lyndon B. Johnson of Texas, introduced the Johnson Amendment, which prohibits nonprofit organizations, including churches, from speaking on political topics which are controversial social issues, such as abortion, homosexuality, etc. Violators could have their tax exemptions revoked. Afraid of the government, many preachers and priests decided or were told by their boards to avoid preaching anything that was controversial. That decision, of course watered down the Bible's message so that it became irrelevant and Christians became lost in the social gospel.

Under U.S. law, the First Amendment guarantees freedom of religion, expression, assembly, and the right to petition, and forbids Congress from restricting an individual's religious practices. But that hasn't stopped persons who oppose Christianity from doing everything they can to prevent participation in it.

Religious discrimination became even more evident and alarming as the 2020 Corona virus pandemic was used as an excuse for eliminating church services and prayer meetings. Officials across the United States took action to stop churchgoers from any form of gatherings. Some governors insisted that liquor stores and abortion providers were essential and should stay open, at the same time issuing citations and threats for anyone who went to church or even parked in a church parking lot.

The mayor of New York announced that he would impose fines or close down buildings of worship if services were held in the city after the COVID-19 outbreak. "No faith tradition endorses anything that endangers the members of that faith. The NYPD, Fire Department, Buildings Department, and everyone has been instructed that if they see worship services going on, they will go to the officials of that congregation, they'll inform them they need to stop the services and disperse."

New York was not alone. In Kansas City, the governor banned religious services of more than 10 people. In Mississippi, the mayor issued an executive order banning all church services. Worshipers, who were practicing social distancing by remaining in their own cars, were given $500.00 fines. The mayor of Louisville, Kentucky said that drive-in church services wouldn't be allowed to happen. From the East Coast to the West Coast, elected officials abused their power in order to restrict people of faith from attending any worship service.

How easily the sheep were scattered!

Chapter 5
WE WILL DESTROY THE FAMILY!

"The second loyalty is to his (the enemy's) family unit, his parents and brothers and sisters. This is destroyed by making a family unit economically non-dependent, by lessening the value of marriage, by making an easiness of divorce and by raising the children wherever possible by the State."

During World War II, when women were needed in the workforce to make up for the men in the military, more American women started working outside the home at paying jobs. Then, after the war, many continued working, making women more independent and men, in danger of losing their role as the essential bread-winners. Having an outside job made it much easier to leave an unloved or unfaithful partner, and because husbands were not always supportive of outside jobs, contributed little to the housework or care of the children, the risk of divorce almost doubled.

At the same time, divorce became easier legally to arrange. Before the twentieth century, divorce statutes in most states were so strict that couples would stay together rather than try to get a divorce. In New York, for instance you had to prove adultery and you had to be a long-term resident of the state. South Carolina allowed no divorce for any reason.

However, America' s political and social climate after World War II, and the prosperity that followed created the unrestrained moral atmosphere that demanded easier divorce. When divorce was easier to obtain and less of a social stigma, more people got divorced.

But the biggest impetus for the destruction of the family was what supposedly was created to help. That was Lyndon Johnson's "War on Poverty." The welfare state that he instigated promoted single-parent homes, the decline of marriage and the break-down of the family. Because the money and benefits paid more if there was no father in the home, many mothers decided that they would rather depend on the government than on a husband with a low-paying job and many couples accepted that it was easier to get divorced than to get a job.

Why stay married when the welfare system penalizes low-income parents who do marry? And if there was no father, the mothers needed more assistance so it became a vicious cycle. Living on welfare became a lifestyle for many women and children, and now more and more men have decided that everyone can live off the government, so why work?

But looking at it from the child's point of view, after a divorce, most mothers have to work full-time, which leaves the children many times without supervision, making them feel abandoned. The custodial parent often is more stressed, less affectionate, and their discipline less consistent and effective, while the non-custodial parent is often less supportive and reliable. Worrying that it is their fault and that they are being punished, children and adolescents often become confused and angry, blaming one parent or both.

Having to move, change schools, accept a step-parent situation, and financial insecurity are just some of the problems that can create resentment. Mental health problems, depression and anxiety rates are found to be higher for children from divorced parents. Conduct disorders, delinquency, impulsive behaviors, trouble in school, a tendency to engage in risky behavior such as substance use and early sexual activity, all are common results of divorce.

> "The role of the psychopolitical operator in this is very strong... He can instruct in an optimum situation the entire nation in how to handle children—and instruct them so that the children, given no control, given no real home, can run wildly about with no responsibility for their actions."

In 1946, Dr. Benjamin Spock's political opponents accused him of teaching "permissiveness" in his book *Baby and Child Care*. They claimed that because he had told parents not to discipline their children, he had ruined an entire generation of American youth. He might not have known and those mothers had no clue, that they were fitting right into the communists' plan. When fathers started leaving it up to the mothers to discipline and train the children, and when experts like Spock started telling mothers to baby the children, the children lost respect for all authority. When divorce became easier and more acceptable, the destruction of the home was imminent.

Communists are "masters of deceit." While most people abhor lying, to communists, lying is a trained pattern of behavior. They encourage any deception that will contribute to their goals. This time they used women.

"There is no way of influencing men so powerfully as by means of the women. These should therefore be our chief study; we should insinuate ourselves into their good opinion, give them hints of emancipation from the tyranny of public opinion, and of standing up for themselves; it will be an immense relief to their enslaved minds to be freed from any one bond of restraint, and it will fire them the more, and cause them to work for us with zeal, without knowing that they do so; for they will only be indulging their own desire of personal admiration" John Robison, *Proofs of a Conspiracy*

Although the right to vote should have always belonged to women as well as men, eventually, the desire of women to become more independent gave rise to women's movements that capitalized on the idea, planted by the media and entertainment industry, that women had not been free and thus needed to be liberated from pleasing their husbands, caring for their children, or even birthing the babies that were in their wombs.

Betty Friedan who wrote The Feminine Mystique and later co-founded the National Organization for Women, insisted that women were not fulfilling their real possibilities by being forced into home-making and child-rearing roles, so she started a movement referred to as "women's liberation."Bella Abzug and Gloria Steinem joined Friedan in founding the National Women's Political Caucus. It continued the erosion of the family unit, the destruction of the institution of marriage and the natural love of mothers toward their children.

The unforeseen result was that women became not only more independent but more uninhibited to the extent that the standards that had once put women on pedestals were torn down by the women themselves. Women's liberation began a whirlpool of degeneracy that men didn't even try to stop.

Although it had been passed by Congress in 1972, the Equal Rights Amendment, (banning any discrimination on the basis of sex,) was prevented from passing and becoming law in all of the states by an organization led by Phyllis Schlafly called STOP ERA.

Schlafly warned women that if that amendment was ensconced in our Constitution that the heterosexual order would be destroyed, morality would be crushed, and women would lose the privileges that women had enjoyed for centuries in the Western world.

"The women's libbers are radicals who are waging a total assault on the family, on marriage, and on children," she said.

However, one year later, feminists celebrated the Supreme Court decision in Roe v. Wade, the landmark ruling that guaranteed a woman's "right" to have an abortion. That effort had been promoted by Margaret Sanger, a eugenicist who founded Planned Parenthood for the express purpose of creating a "master race." She intended to do that by lowering the birthrate of "inferiors" such as the poor, the handicapped, and racial minorities. These are only three of her quotes but they reveal the wicked roots of the abortion movement and expose the demonic mindset behind what you see in movies, music and social attitudes, a culture of death. By researching what she said and what she wrote, it is apparent that Sanger hated children, parenthood, marriage, and minorities.

1. "But for my view, I believe that there should be no more babies."— Interview with John Parsons, 1947

2. "The most merciful thing that the large family does to one of its infant members is to kill it."— *Woman and the New Race*, Chapter 5, "The Wickedness of Creating Large Families." (1920) http://www.bartleby.com/1013/

3. "We don't want the word to go out that we want to exterminate the Negro population..."— Letter to Dr. Clarence J. Gamble, December 10, 1939, p. 2 https://libex.smith.edu/omeka/...

It is incomprehensible that women would want to kill their own babies, yet that is what over sixty million American mothers have done. We thought Hitler's Holocaust was insanity! Commercials on television are always asking you to save the animals but when have you seen one that asked you to save the babies? No, you will not see that commercial because it isn't "politically correct" to save babies.

It is just another example of pressure from the top combined with pressure from the bottom. The "elites" have used the population-control programs supported by the United Nations and government-funded organizations such as Planned Parenthood to create the lie that abortion is a woman's right and have talked the masses into believing it. China's forced abortion program exemplifies the real agenda, which is to reduce the population, especially of certain ethnicities and social levels.

The women's movement and the abortion program were not enough to destroy homes completely, so people were encouraged by the entertainment industry to get involved in adultery, casual sex and sexual immorality of all kinds, regardless of Biblical laws on sexual behavior. One of the goals of the ACLU and the Communists was to get the U.S. Supreme Court to overturn the federal Defense of Marriage Act and to abolish marriage as we know it. The result has been complete confusion, with men and women pretending to be different sexes and children being tossed back and forth, not knowing what to believe.

Chapter 6
WE WILL DESTROY YOUR YOUTH!

"Under the saccharine guise of assistance to them, rigorous child labor laws are the best means to deny the child any right in the society. By refusing to let him earn, by forcing him into unwanted dependence upon a grudging parent, by making certain in other channels that the parent is never in other than economic stress, the child can be driven in his teens into revolt. Delinquency will ensue."

From the earliest days of the United States, efforts were made to curtail child labor. Stories of the abuse of children working for long hours in dangerous jobs for little pay was so heart wrenching and evil that it made you wonder how employers could allow it, but they did, until educational reformers and labor organizers, who had other agendas, began fighting it.

In 1836, Massachusetts became the first to pass an actual law prohibiting children under fifteen years of age from working in factories. That law also required children to attend school for at least three hours per day. Six years later, again Massachusetts led the way by limiting working hours for children to ten hours per day.

At the beginning of the twentieth century, people became more intense about the idea that childhood should be reserved for play and education, and when labor unions came into existence, it hastened the end of most child labor because, not only could they object based on moral grounds but also on economic grounds, since adult jobs were often given to children who would work for cheaper wages.

In 1933, Congress passed the National Industrial Recovery Act as part of President Franklin Roosevelt's New Deal. Child labor was outlawed in most industries besides agriculture and domestic work. It was the Great Depression and thousands of positions that had been filled by children were now needed for unemployed adults.

Although the NRA was declared unconstitutional in 1935, Roosevelt came back with the Fair Labor Standards Act in 1938 which made the minimum wage, maximum hours and anti-child labor provisions set out in the NRA permanent. This law regulates the days, hours, and times that 14,

15, 16, and 17-year old employees can work. Children under age 14 cannot work any non-agricultural jobs unless employed by their parents in a non-hazardous industry. Children ages 14-15 can only work hours when they are not in school. There are also rules about how many hours they can work each day.

When government enacts good laws, they tend to push them to limits unforeseen by those who instigated them. The government recently tried to make a law that children could not even work on their family farms, but enough people found out about it and started raising so many objections that they had to back down.

Many people have forgotten that work is good for children, especially teenagers who need to stay busy to keep from getting into trouble. Many teens have learned more and gotten ahead faster doing a good hard job than they could have with a mediocre education. Why should children and youth think that they must wait to live and work until they have finished college? Many of our forefathers had received a quality education by the time they were fourteen and most had been working from a young age.

"By making readily available drugs of various kinds, by giving the teenager alcohol, by praising his wildness, by stimulating him with sex literature and advertising to him or her practices as taught at the Sexpol, the psychopolitical operator can create the necessary attitude of chaos, idleness and worthlessness into which can then be cast the solution which will give the teenager complete freedom everywhere—Communism."

Do these not sound familiar? Stimulating the teenager with sex literature? In Ashcroft v. Free Speech Coalition (2002), the Supreme Court overturned an act of Congress, the Child Pornography Protection Act, on the grounds that prohibiting computer-generated images of children engaging in sex acts was an overly broad definition of pornography and a violation of the First Amendment.

The theater and TV screen have become molders of values and social behavior in our society, to the extent that the programs and movies we see today become tomorrow's standards. As far back as 1971, the average film contained thirty-eight scenes of violence and sex, including nudity, illicit sex, physical aggression, slaughter, and massacre. In 43 percent of the films the heroes were portrayed as law breakers or antisocial characters. This was in 1971.

"Sexual lust, masochism, and any other desirable perversion can be induced by pain-drug hypnosis and the benefit of Psychopolitics."

Documentation shows that television's erotic influence is so pervasive that it increases sexual activity in teens and younger children. Studies show that the age of first sexual intercourse significantly decreases due to the influence of TV. The more television watched the lower the age for that first sexual encounter. Not only do studies show it, children themselves report that television encourages them to take part in sexual activity at a young age.

The acceptance of gay characters is partly a reflection of our society's changing attitudes toward the gay community and partly a product of TV's influence. There have been numerous studies showing that when people watch shows with gay characters in them, they hold on to fewer negative gay prejudices, exactly what the liberals had planned.

"The psychopolitical operative "should pay particular attention to the "forgetter mechanism" aspect of hypnotism, which is to say, implantation in the unconscious mind.

In 1972, the Surgeon General's Office of the United States National Institutes of Health announced that a number of behavioral studies showed a causal link between the exposure of children to televised violence and their subsequent aggressive behavior. At about the same time a researcher at the University of Utah showed that children who had been heavily exposed to violence on TV could also become desensitized to violence, illustrated by the phenomenon known as "bystander apathy," where people seem willing to stand by and watch while others are injured or killed, doing nothing to help the victim.

To produce a new behavior in a person, you need only show him a televised model of this behavior over and over in emotional or attractive conditions, and they will begin to imitate it. Psychologists have concluded that imitative learning can manipulate people's values, thereby playing a highly influential role in accelerating social changes. Television and motion pictures have significant power to persuade and change behavior. Since movie censorship is nearly nonexistent, almost anything can be filmed and shown on the screen. Violence, sadism, sex, great varieties of antisocial behaviors, and modeling the glamorized use of drugs are just a few of the incessant themes that have been repeatedly performed to influence our children.

Children and adolescents are particularly vulnerable to the messages conveyed through television, Many cannot discriminate between what they see and what is real. In the scientific literature on media violence, the connection of media violence to real-life aggressive behavior and violence has been substantiated. Just one example is a long-term study between 1977 and 1992 which looked at 557 children from five countries and their TV viewing habits and revisited them as young adults. The study found that early exposure to TV violence as children was a predictor of aggressive behavior later on. This was true even when the study controlled for socio-economic factors, parenting styles and children who showed aggressive tendencies early on.

In 2001, the American Academy of Pediatrics expressed its concerns about the amount of time children and adolescents spent viewing television and the content of what they view. Various surveys have shown that most children watch TV from fourteen to forty-nine hours a week, depending on age and socio-economic level. With the ever present cell phone, you can multiply that several times.

One study notes that the average child in the U.S. has witnessed over 10,000 murders on TV by the age of fourteen. Under the influence of television, the frontal lobe cannot function at its full capacity and it no longer critically analyzes the information. Terrible scenes can be depicted, but the viewer tends only to laugh or shrug them off. Normally, if those kinds of events happened in real life the individual would be appalled. Even this is changing as people become more desensitized through exposure. Hitler brainwashed his troops that way.

As for drugs and alcohol use, half of America's high school seniors have tried an illicit drug by the time they graduate and four in 10 have used it in just the past year and teen alcohol statistics show that 11% of all alcohol consumed in the United States is consumed by those aged 12 to 20. By the end of high school, teenage alcohol statistics tell us that 72% of students will have consumed alcohol.

Teens who drink alcohol are more likely to experience: school, social, and legal problems, such as arrest for driving or physically hurting someone while drunk, alcohol-related car crashes, unprotected sexual activity, physical and sexual assault, higher risk for suicide and homicide, and abuse of other drugs.

Substance abuse can affect virtually every one of the body's systems. Examples of this include permanent brain damage. Juveniles who use drugs are more likely to have unprotected sex, sex with a stranger, some kind of sexual activity. This, in turn, puts them at risk for pregnancy, rape commission or victimization, and for sexually transmitted diseases. Substance use can cause other emotional problems like anxiety, depression, mood swings, or hallucinations, any one of which can result in death by suicide or homicide.

As anyone who turns on a television set can see, children and teenagers continue to be bombarded with programming full of sexual imagery, violence, and glorification of alcohol, and illicit drugs. It is very apparent that the corrupters of our society have used movies, television, music, pornography, the internet, etc. to very effectively hypnotize and brainwash the youth of America.

Chapter 7
WE WILL CORRUPT CAMPAIGNS TO IMPROVE YOUTH!

"Movements to improve youth should be invaded and corrupted, as this might interrupt campaigns to produce in youth delinquency, addiction, drunkenness, and sexual promiscuity."

Research summarized by the U.S. Centers for Disease Control and Prevention indicates the following:

- Approximately one in four girls and one in six boys are sexually abused before the age of 18.

- Most victims suffer the abuse at the hands of someone they know, often a trusted adult.

- Pedophiles are often drawn to positive youth settings, such as schools, scouting, or sports, because such environments bring them into contact with so many potential targets.

The ACLU had fought an on-going battle with the Boy Scouts of America to force them to accept scout leaders who practice homosexual behavior. In 2015, the governing body of the Boy Scouts of America voted to end its decades-long ban on gay scout leaders. The organization's national executive board, concluded that the policy of excluding gay adults "was no longer legally defensible." The decision was approved by 79 percent of the board.

This was after the Boy Scouts had identified, in the years between 1944 and 2016, more than 12,000 victims of sexual abuse. The Boy Scouts of America believed more than 7,800 of its former leaders were involved in sexually abusing children over the course of 72 years, about 2,800 more leaders than previously known publicly. So they made it legal.

When that wasn't enough for their far-left agenda, the ACLU started suing the BSA over the Three "G's"—Gays, Godless, and Girls—hoping to force the organization to allow homosexuals, atheists, and girls to join. Other left-wing organizations did the same and eventually the BSA officials succumbed to the politics of inclusion, eliminating their traditional standards to appease the critics.

However, the ACLU and the Homosexual movement never stop at one success. They want to continue expanding and taking over every territory. The only one of the Three "G's" that the BSA held the line on were the atheists. But even there, the organization that prided itself on honoring the Judeo-Christian ethos deleted all requirements and allowed anyone to join who professed a belief in anything, ranging from witches to Wiccans.

The Boy Scouts were not the first youth organization to identify sexual abuse in their midst. In recent years, hundreds, if not thousands, of individuals have come forward claiming sexual abuse from priests in the Roman Catholic Church. Numerous "pedophile priests" have been identified. Most of the time, rather than removing priests from the priesthood, the Catholic Church in most instances attempted to cover up the sexual abuse by transferring the offenders to different parishes. The scandal and attempted cover-up is on-going and reaches all the way to the papacy itself.

In Protestant denominations, questions about physical and sexual abuse drew widespread attention in 2018 when a former missionary was charged with sexual assault of a child under 17. His alleged abuse of a teenage girl occurred as he served in youth ministry in a church. Similar accounts of other former youth ministers also made headlines in the last year. Not to leave any organizations out, the world of sports was horrified to learn of the abuse of young U.S. gymnasts by their team physician. More than 150 women testified against him in the trial that resulted in his conviction.

The Communists have been very successful in their campaigns to corrupt every organization meant to improve youth. We American citizens have been asleep or very naïve but, now that we are awake, we must start fighting for our children and our country.

Chapter 8
WE WILL DESTROY THE EDUCATION SYSTEM!

"Those who expect to be ignorant and free expect what never was and never will be." —Thomas Jefferson

WASHINGTON—U.S Secretary of Education Betsy DeVos released the following statement on the 2019 National Assessment of Educational Progress (NAEP) results:

> "Every American family needs to open The Nation's Report Card this year and think about what it means for their child and for our country's future. The results are, frankly, devastating. This country is in a student achievement crisis, and over the past decade it has continued to worsen, especially for our most vulnerable students.

> "Two out of three of our nation's children aren't proficient readers. In fact, fourth grade reading declined in 17 states and eighth grade reading declined in 31. The gap between the highest and lowest performing students is widening, despite $1 trillion in Federal spending over 40 years designated specifically to help close it.

> "This must be America's wake-up call. We cannot abide these poor results any longer. We can neither excuse them away nor simply throw more money at the problem."

In our nation's capital, a stunning two-thirds of residents over the age of 15 are classified as functionally illiterate, according to a report by the State Education Agency. (I'm wondering where Congressional members fall in those statistics. It would explain their inability to balance the budget or to get anything else done.)

In 2017, the Huffington Post reported, "Students in Shanghai who recently took international exams for the first time outscored every other school system in the world. In the same test, American students ranked 25th in math, 17th in science and 14th in reading."

In 2018, the U.S. Department of Education released the results of its National Assessment of Educational Progress (NAEP) proving that the majority of American children are not proficient in reading or math. Not reading and math, but reading or math. In some districts, eight out of 100 students were proficient in neither. In California, their own testing showed that more than half of the students in every grade except the 11th failed the standards, the lowest they had been in decades.

American government schools are mass-producing illiterate citizens while charging American taxpayers more than a trillion dollars per year for the service.

Why should this be happening? How did we get to this level of illiteracy?

Long before government seized control over education, Americans were incredibly well-educated and vast amounts of evidence from that era show that literacy levels were significantly higher in the mid-to-late 1700 than they are today. Tax-funded k-12 government schools would have been inconceivable to Americans from the 1600s to the mid-1899s, especially education without the Bible and God. Learning to read in order to read the Bible and to become good citizens was the purpose for education. But not all were thinking of religious reasons for developing a system of government schools.

There was actually a long-term plan by Robert Owen and others in a communist commune in Indiana called "New Harmony," who rejected Christianity and who were determined to remake society. The Owenites wanted government schools to take over child rearing from the earliest possible ages so that by segregating the children into classes by age, it would allow them to more easily control and mold them into more obedient citizens.

There was also a lawyer, Horace Mann, who became famous for educational reform, although he had almost no experience as an educator. He and his wealthy backers worked to expand the size of government and to take over the nations' educational program. One of their primary goals was to ensure that everyone was equal in every way and to destroy the Christian roots of education. But strangely, there was an increase of crime and immorality everywhere that government schools were started.

The methods used to teach reading in government schools today was a failure over 150 years ago when Mann first tried it in Boston. Rudolf Flesch tried to alert the public when he wrote in his 1955 book, *Why Johnny Can't Read*, that children were being forced to memorize "sight words" instead of being taught phonics, producing life-long reading disabilities in tens of millions of American children.

Does it seem strange to anyone that our children attend school for thirteen years and many of them graduate without knowing how to read, write, spell, or do basic math calculations? Most of them cannot tell you about our American heritage, our anatomy, what is in the Constitution, or where India is on a map. Perish the thought that they would be able to reason, debate or know how to make informed decisions. Not because they are not intelligent. Not because they do not want to learn. And it is not because we do not have good teachers. Most of our teachers are terribly frustrated about not being able to teach so that students will love to learn. We are producing illiterate citizens because we refuse to change the educational system to fit the needs of the students instead of the convenience and ideas of the educational elite.

All children are naturally curious and want to learn until they are educated out of it. Children come into the world with great creative talent and we should recognize and develop those abilities but that doesn't mean they must all be the same. Every child is different, learns differently and learns at different speeds. Thirteen years of education should give us the most intelligent, innovative citizens in the world but most innovators had to get out of the public schools to be able to learn and develop their abilities. Unless they have really good, unhampered teachers, most of our students are either frustrated or bored and they haven't the background knowledge to even know why.

More time is being spent trying to make sure that every child is on the same level than is spent challenging each child to learn as much as he can. More time is spent on discipline and paperwork than is spent on developing motivating lessons. There is so much to learn and we literally waste thirteen years of our children's lives!

Do not think for a minute that our country's free education is for the purpose of giving all children a quality education. It is not so that every child will have a good education. It is so that every child will have the same education. Our public schools are instituted to keep children at the same level and to make certain that all children grow up to be pliable, non-thinking citizens who can be molded and shaped to do whatever their leaders want them to do, a nation of people who do not know and perhaps do not care what is happening to America as long as the government will take care of them.

That is why we have government schools, to brainwash an uneducated people into complacency. Our government leaders want American citizens who would rather view "reality" television or endless ball games than to read and discuss intelligent ideas. They could not control a citizenry who can think for themselves.

John Stuart Mill (1806–73) was the most influential English language philosopher of the nineteenth century. With his education supervised by his father, he learned Greek at age three, Latin at age eight, and by age twelve had absorbed most of the classics, along with algebra, Euclid, and history. In his early teenage years, he studied political economy, logic, and calculus, using his spare time to investigate experimental science. Little wonder that he made this observation:

> "A general State Education is a mere contrivance for moulding people to be exactly like one another, and as the mould in which it casts them is that which pleases the dominant power in the government,… it establishes a despotism (tyranny) over the mind…"

Americans have been taught, but not at school. They have been taught by TV, technology and their peers. At school, they have been brain-washed. They know little about civics, their heritage or economic principles. Our textbooks are filled with misinterpretations of history. The same people who make billions testing students have already made billions producing textbooks that were so slanted and incomplete, that teachers who were not brain-washed themselves were alarmed at the contents.

Universities are famously left-leaning because teachers are taught the ideology of progressive socialism, and then sent to further indoctrinate students. The Department of Education spends millions of dollars to mandate "No Child Left Behind" to make sure that all children are on the same level. The Texas Education Agency spends hundreds of millions on tests to make sure that all students are learning the same things. Then local school administrators spend hundreds of thousands so that all students learn the same thing at the same time in the same way.

What a priceless cookie-cutter education system we have! But that will produce what we evidently want, teachers who are not allowed to think, children who cannot think and a society that will not think, but will willingly follow whatever the government tells them to do.

School has become a joke. No one who has worked in it lately can ever refer to it as an educational system. A system, yes, educational, not so much. It is a government program and you know what happens when the government runs anything, especially after they kicked God out, which is exactly what happened.

In a book entitled *The Naked Communist*, number 28 of 45 objectives of the Communists plan to destroy America is: "Eliminate prayer or any phase of religious expression in the schools on the ground that it violates the principle of 'separation of church and state.'" We played right into their hands and got it straight out of their playbook.

Their objective was accomplished in 1963, with the help of Madalyn Murray O'Hair, an American atheist. The Communist Leadership saw in her a chance to do away with all things Christian and, with the assistance of the American Civil Liberties Union, they took it to the Supreme Court, which was filled with left-wing liberals.

On June 17, 1963, the Supreme Court, by an overwhelming majority vote of 8 to 1, ruled that Bible reading and prayers in school were unconstitutional. The thoughts of the Founding Fathers, who wrote the **Constitution** *and the* **Bill of Rights**, who created schools for the express purpose of being able to read, and especially to read the Bible, were ignored. For 343 years school prayer and Bible reading had been an everyday part of American life. It was suddenly declared unconstitutional.

Communists have invaded our courts and our schools: In 1962, Engel vs. Vitale, the Court held that public school teachers could not open class with a prayer. In Murray v. Curlett (1963), schools could not require passages from the Bible be read or that the Lord's Prayer be recited in public schools at the beginning of the school day. In 1963, School District of Abington Township vs. Schemp said that the state could not require the recitation of the Lord's Prayer and the reading of Scripture in public schools. In Stone v. Graham (1980), the Court struck down a Kentucky law requiring that the Ten Commandments be posted in public-school classrooms.

In 1985, Wallace vs. Jaffree, the Court ruled that a moment of silence was unconstitutional because it was intended to convey a message of state approval of prayer activities in public schools. In Lee v. Weisman (1992), the Court ruled that clergy may not lead prayers at public-school events.

In 2000, the Court overruled a Texas law allowing high school students to pray at athletic events. And in 2002, the 9th Circuit Court of Appeals ruled that reciting the Pledge of Allegiance in public schools was an unconstitutional endorsement of religion, because it contains the words "under God."

Public schools were barred from showing a film about the settlement of Jamestown because the film depicted the erection of a cross at the settlement. In Alaska, students were told they could not use the word "Christmas" in school because it had the word "Christ" in it. In Virginia, a federal court ruled that while a homosexual newspaper may be distributed on a high school campus, religious newspapers may not. In Colorado, a music teacher was stopped from singing traditional Christmas carols in her classes. The courts have declared that if a student prays over his lunch, it is unconstitutional for him to pray aloud.

The ACLU have produced countless law suits to get prayer and Bible reading removed from public schools. They have sued school boards and cities across the country in an effort to remove all traces of God from American society. They demanded removal of the Ten Commandments from schools, court houses and public parks, crosses from War Memorials, Christmas displays, etc. They claim that anything Christian is in violation of the "Separation of Church and State" clause. There is no such clause in the U.S. Constitution. **You will find it however, in the constitution of the old Soviet Union.**

When I was in South Africa, the children in the public schools were singing, "Jesus loves me." When I told them that we in America could no longer do that, one of the high school girls asked me two questions: "Is that true?" and "Why did you let it happen?" That is what I am wondering as I write this book. How did this happen in America? Why did we allow it to happen? What are we going to do about it?

Some time ago, a mother packed a Bible verse in her son's lunch box. He read it at lunch. Other children gathered around to hear it. A teacher said it violated the "separation of church and state," so the seven-year –old was told to take it off the school grounds. Still children came to hear. When that didn't stop the boy, a sheriff's deputy showed up at the boy's home and warned the parents that because "someone might be offended," their child was to keep his Bible verses to himself. This was not in Russia or China or Iran. This was in Los Angeles, California. This was in America.

We now live in an era where public school students may define their own gender and use the bathroom that matches that identity, but they can't read Bible verses to their classmates upon request.

Abraham Lincoln said,

"The philosophy of the class room in one generation will be the philosophy of government in the next.

Chapter 9
WE WILL INFILTRATE THE HIGHEST CIRCLES OF YOUR GOVERNMENT!

"All lands are governed by the few and only pretend to consult with the many. It is no different in America. The petty official, the maker of laws alike can be made to believe the worst. It is not necessary to convince the masses. It is only necessary to work incessantly upon the official, using personal defamations, wild lies, false evidences and constant propaganda to make him fight for you."

There should be a special place reserved for people like Adam Schiff, who can lie over and over with a straight face and Nancy Pelosi who led the charge to attack Trump without any evidence of criminality. And we, the American people desperately hope that the Clintons will get what they deserve. It leaves a bad taste in your mouth when you see them literally getting by with murder multiple times and never having to answer for any of their crimes. Lying to everyone for so long has them convinced that justice will never find them.

In every decade, the underground Communists, Illuminists, Bilderburgs, members of the Trilateral Commission, and the Council on Foreign Relations, etc. have found representatives from all parts of society to infiltrate our legislative bodies and political lobbies in order to fill our government agencies with corrupt schemers who are intent on producing a "One World Government."

But it isn't just Democrats. Many Republicans have also been guilty of working toward that end. Examine both parties, Democrats and Republicans, and you can be assured that this part of the socialist/communist/satanic plan is working well. That is why we feel so helpless and why so many voters feel disenfranchised, because it always seems that, no matter whom we put in office, they turn out to be just like the ones already there and do nothing differently than what the others have been doing, watching out for themselves instead of the country.

As far back as 1957, George W. Malone, a U.S. senator from Nevada, speaking before Congress, warned,

"I believe that if the people of this nation fully understood what Congress has done to them over the last 49 years, they would move on Washington; they would not wait for an election...It adds up to a preconceived plan to destroy the economic and social independence of the United States!"

The constant attack on gun ownership through legislation, the progressive lack of respect for states' rights by both political parties, and the assault on our First Amendment rights are but a few examples. It may be too late to regain control of the government but there is no chance unless the American people begin to take an active role in it and insist that those we elect vote to abide by the Constitution and reduce the size of a government that has grown into a monster that will destroy the country.

That is why Donald Trump was elected president in 2016. None of us had any confidence in the people we had in Washington. We wanted someone who was not a politician, who would try to "drain the swamp."

A perfect example of infiltration is the Democratic Party. The wave of socialist Congressmen as well as Muslims who have no regard for this country should speak to the fact that people are trying to overturn our government. Even now, there is a scheme to allow convicts, illegal aliens and dead people to register to vote.

Many examples could be given of elected officials ignoring laws they have sworn to uphold. But some recent examples are so brazen that you wonder how the constituents of that state or county would allow it. One district attorney fired 31 prosecutors during his first week on the job, calling for an end to "mass incarceration." Several governors have stopped arresting people for "insignificant" crimes such as selling drugs or theft. In New York City, rioters broke into stores, vandalized and stole and, when arrested, immediately were freed because of a "no-bail" law in N.Y.

"It is not too much to hope that psycho-political operatives would... in a country such as the United States, become the most intimate advisors to political figures, even to the point of advising the entirety of a political party as to its actions in an election. The long view is the important view."

Because spies and infiltrators are everywhere, we have to look at the "foxes in the hen house;" not only, "Who were the presidents?" but, "Who were his advisors?" Who surrounded Obama when he was president? Were any of them corrupt? Were they socialist? Were they communist? Did they have another agenda besides the good of the American people?

Ten of them, including President Obama himself made the 2012 **"Most Corrupt" List** compiled by Judicial Watch, an organization which investigates official corruption. Some items investigated were unconstitutional executive orders to expand illegal immigration, parts of Obama Care, and taxpayer money going to Wall Street banks. They were also looking into the government funding of the "criminal ACORN network," as well as the use of unaccountable "czars" — many of whom were put in charge of major government programs and have been linked to "scandals, thefts, kickbacks, conflicts of interest, and radical leftist policies,"

With Obama that year in the top ten most corrupt politicians in Washington were: Secretary of State, Hillary Clinton and UN Ambassador, Susan Rice, because of their lies about Benghazi; disgraced Attorney General Eric Holder and the "Fast and Furious" gun-running scandal; Secretary of Health and Human Services, Kathleen Sebelius, a radical pro-abortion official; Secretary of Energy Steven Chu and the Solyndra scandal; and Van Jones, Obama's "Green Jobs Czar," a self-proclaimed communist.

If we had been taught history, we might have learned our lesson about examining our officials by remembering Algier Hiss, a confidant of President Franklin Roosevelt. He was a former U.S. State Department official and a favorite of Franklin Roosevelt and the Democrats of that century. He was also a Soviet spy.

Being Roosevelt's right-hand man, he was at Yalta in February of 1945, where the postwar boundaries of Europe were being drawn and he was the one that arranged for most of Eastern Europe to be placed under Communist rule. Years after Hiss's trial for espionage had been forgotten, it was found that he had passed crucial information to the Soviets for more than a decade. The secret had been well kept by the media and the "progressives" (Communists) in the Democratic Party.

Hiss not only turned Eastern Europe over to Stalin, he also positioned himself to be one of the architects of the United Nations.

The world does not realize how many Marxist lies we have swallowed, even believing that the Soviet Union "collapsed" and that the West won the Cold War. But, if we had listened to **Mikhail Gorbachev, Nov. 2, 1987, when he addressed the Soviet Politburo**, we would have known, because he said,

"In October 1917, we parted with the old world, rejecting it once and for all. We are moving toward a new world, the world of Communism. We shall never turn off that road!" He continued, "Comrades, do not be concerned about all that you hear about glasnost and perestroika and democracy in the coming years. These are primarily for outward consumption. There will be no significant internal change within the Soviet Union other than for cosmetic purposes. Our purpose is to disarm the Americans and let them fall asleep."

The Communist Party USA celebrated their 100th anniversary in 2019. Their goals are the same as those of the Communist Party everywhere – the overthrow of all existing free governments and the establishment of a Marxist world order. They are not alone. They have secret conspirators behind the scenes. The media, the entertainment industry, and the courts are all working together to see how quickly the moral degeneration will reduce us to third-world status and perhaps even to nuclear ashes. Their puppets in the media have made Americans afraid to be labeled intolerant when they oppose anything that the left wing is promoting, and called hysterical if they talk of conspiracy or communism. Determined to wipe out American independence, they have done a very good job of making Americans ashamed of defending their own freedoms.

In order to control the public, communists use words like "equality," "tolerance," "my body, my choice," "white supremacists," "racists," and "peace" to promote conflict and division. They create a victim mind set in different groups, women, blacks, Hispanics, homosexuals, etc., telling them that they are "oppressed" and encouraging them to fight the "whites" or the "religious bigots" or the authorities, claiming to be protestors for the mistreated. Their real purpose, as always, is to use them to create chaos everywhere.

Often the communist leaders team up with the Democratic Party but they get their orders not just from Moscow or Beijing, but from the very rich, very powerful bankers and billionaires, like the Rockefellers, Bill Gates, Soros, and Zuckerberg, who are manipulating world events. After watching the Democrats try to destroy the presidency of Donald Trump through false Russian collusion investigations and failed one-party impeachment trials, it is very apparent that spies have infiltrated the highest levels of our bureaucracy and government, from the Justice Department to the FBI, CIA, Homeland Security, etc. Just looking at a few instances of corruption, from the spying to the lying, the Democratic Party and, quite often the Republican Party as well, have been unashamedly in bed with the media, the Communists, and the wealthy saboteurs who want to take down this nation.

Chapter 10
WE WILL TAKE OVER YOUR COURTS!

"We will use the courts, use the judges, use the Constitution of the country, use its medical societies and its laws to further our ends."

The motto of the United States of America is not hard to find. "In God We Trust" is on every dollar bill and every little dime and penny. Many of our schools and government buildings have it inscribed in the masonry. The Pledge of Allegiance recited in public schools describes the U.S. as "one nation under God."

Although our Christian heritage and traditions accompanying it have lasted for more than 200 years, these traditions have been constantly challenged in the past 60 years by the ACLU, which has had willing accomplices in the judges of the courts to destroy the foundation on which America was built.

The Founding Fathers established the separation of powers: Congress, (the legislative branch) is responsible for passing laws, the president (the executive branch) is responsible for governance according to those executing and enforcing laws, and the Supreme Court (the judicial branch). having neither the power to pass laws nor to govern, originally had the least power, but has now usurped the power of the Congress and has been allowed to change laws as well as the meaning of the Constitution.

Communists found that they could fill government agencies and Congress with leftists to take control of the legislative process and they could influence the judicial branch with their own judges, prosecutors, or other officials responsible for carrying out the laws. Their strategy is not to amend the Constitution, but to change the original meaning of the words to match any progressive ideology that they hold.

As elected representatives of the people, members of Congress and the president serve at the pleasure of the people and can be removed if they go against public opinion. On the other hand, Supreme Court justices don't need to satisfy any constituents, since they hold their positions for life. And it is much easier to influence the decisions of nine people than it is to change the mindset of the population.

Of course, lawyers greatly influence court rulings and Communist lawyers have been able to infiltrate these proceedings disguised as a legal association, pretending to guarantee our freedoms when in reality their sole purpose is to remove our liberties and to destroy America. The American Civil Liberties Union, the ACLU, has as its basic training the art of creating and repeating lies so often that they are assumed to be the truth.

The ACLU was based on the Communist Manifesto which was promoted by spies such as Emma Goldman. A promoter of anarchism, radical education, free love, and birth control, she was deported to Russia, but not before her ideas assisted in the founding of the American Civil Liberties Union. Louis Francis Budenz, along with William Z. Foster, and Elizabeth Gurley Flynn, became prominent leaders of the Communist Party, USA, and started the organization in 1920 that has almost single-handedly overturned all that made America great. (Budenz later broke with the Communist Party in 1945 and became a militant anti-Communist.)

Goldman also influenced Roger Baldwin, who in 1935, became the long-time director of the ACLU. She taught him to mask his true agenda so that the elites would fund the very same organization that was working to destroy the free enterprise system that led to the creation of their wealth. Baldwin voiced his views in the Harvard reunion book ... by declaring:

"I am for socialism, disarmament, and ultimately for abolishing the state itself…Communism is the goal."

Baldwin, pretending loyalty to the nation, told his followers to "steer away from making it look like a socialist enterprise. We want to look like patriots in everything we do." He used that strategy to occasionally defend a conservative cause, thereby promoting the pretense that the organization was nonpartisan, while systematically weakening the framework of America. This organization has contributed massively to the decline of America by promoting sexual perversion and abortion and, at the same time, stripping Bible reading, prayer, and the Ten Commandments from our schools and courthouses.

In the 1947 case, Everson vs. Board of Education, Justice Hugo Black, a former KuKlux Klan member stated, "First Amendment has erected a wall between church and state. That wall must be kept high and impregnable." The wording is found nowhere in the U.S. Constitution, but it was proposed to the court by the ACLU.

It was based on a letter that the Danbury Baptist Association of Danbury, Connecticut, wrote to President Jefferson because of a rumor that a particular denomination was soon to be recognized as the national denomination. On January 1, 1802, President Jefferson responded to them in a letter to assure them that the federal government would not establish any single denomination of Christianity as the national denomination:

"I contemplate with solemn reverence that act of the whole American people which declared that their legislature should "make no law respecting an establishment of religion, or prohibiting the free exercise thereof, "thus building a wall of separation between Church and State."

Anyone who reads about the authors of the Constitution would know that they intended freedom of religion, not freedom from religion. Indeed, Thomas Jefferson himself said,

"Can the liberties of a nation be secure when we have removed the conviction that these liberties are the gift of God."

Before that 1947 Court, the Court had not only refused to separate religious principles, but had relied on those principles when rendering its decisions In People v. Ruggles, they wrote:

"The morality of the country is deeply engrafted upon Christianity....(we are) people whose manners...and whose morals have been elevated and inspired ...by means of the Christian religion."

We Christians have been denied our rights. We are not allowed to have the Ten Commandments or nativity scenes in public places. We are not supposed to sing about Christ at Christmas programs. We are not supposed to take our Bibles into the schools or our offices. We are not supposed to pray in school. (Frankly, our schools need all of the prayer they can get.) We are not supposed to pray before ballgames or graduation ceremonies.

Our children and our grandchildren will pay the price not only for the economic ruin that our government is pushing us into, but also the infringement of our freedoms. The free enterprise system is being replaced by the free welfare system. The incentive to work hard is being replaced by the "You owe me" society.

The national anthem, national motto, Pledge of Allegiance, are all under siege by atheists and leftist activists to remove "under God" from all of them.

The Supreme Court (the judicial branch of the government) has neither the power to pass laws nor to govern. Even though the Congress, which is the legislative branch legitimately responsible for passing laws, reflected the opinion of the American public and voted to retain the phrase, the courts are still overturning the rights of Christians all over America. President Trump is the first president to start defending our first amendment liberties.

The Court invaded our schools. The rejection of school prayer was not the first but the most flagrant abuse of our First Amendment rights and the most obvious take-over of society, a new hostility toward religion. This was the prayer that was struck down in Engel v. Vitale: "Almighty God, we acknowledge our dependence upon Thee, and we beg Thy blessings upon us, our parents, our teachers and our country. Amen.

The Court invaded our homes: In 1973, seven of the nine justices decided that the so-called "right to personal privacy' includes unrestricted access to abortion. Roe vs. Wade set the stage for the killing of unborn children by legalized abortion up to the moment of birth. More than 60 million Americans, (more than the entire population of the states of California and New York ,) have been sacrificed on the altar of "choice."

The "Freedom of Choice Act" which bars federal government regulation of abortion, defied public polls, by an act of Congress and a President, and the ruling of the Supreme Court. This was co-sponsored by Hillary Clinton, Boxer, Nadler, and others. In 2000, the Supreme Court struck down Nebraska's law banning partial-birth abortion. Thus, full-term, healthy babies who would otherwise be delivered kicking and squirming are killed as they come down the birth canal.

We have to stand up and say, "Stop! We, the People, will not stand for it any longer. You are our servants, not our dictators. We can replace you and we will do so if you do not start listening to the majority instead of the influential few."

The courts turned society upside down. Everything that we called virtue, they have dismantled and declared that right was wrong and wrong was right.

"By releasing continued propaganda on the subject of dope addiction, homosexuality, and depraved conduct on the part of the young, even the judges of a country can become suborned into reacting violently against the youth of the country…"

In 1996, in Romer vs. Evans , when the voters of Colorado overwhelmingly passed an amendment to the Colorado Constitution to ensure that those who practice homosexual behavior would not receive special legal rights and privileges beyond that of ordinary citizens, the ACLU and the homosexual activists sued the state. The Court ruled that the Colorado amendment displayed ill will for homosexuals and violated the Equal Protection Clause of the Fourteenth Amendment. In 2003, Lawrence vs. Texas provided constitutional protections to homosexual sodomy. Justice Anthony Kennedy said we have to look at "foreign law."And in May, 2008, the California Supreme Court declared same-sex "marriage" legal in Cal., overturning a statewide initiative that clearly defined marriage as exclusively between a man and a woman.

The court **defended** the distribution of child pornography and supported lawsuits against laws to protect children from registered sex offenders. In 1982, in New York vs. Ferber - The ACLU asked the justices to decree that child pornography was protected by the Constitution. While the Court rejected that argument, in 2004 Ashcroft vs. ACLU, the Supreme Court prevented the implementation of the Child Online Protection Act, which was designed to protect minors from obscene material on the Internet.

The U.S. Supreme Court and state and district courts are removing our religious freedoms. The courts work to prevent Christians and ministries from publicly sharing the Gospel at various times and places—especially during the Christmas season.

In 2005, the U.S. Supreme Court ruled that the display of the Ten Commandments in a state courthouse was unconstitutional and must be removed. The Freedom from Religion Foundation is suing Congress to remove "under God" from the Pledge of Allegiance. The so-called "Fairness Doctrine" would force Christian broadcasters to "balance" programs with equal time for opposing opinion.

Freedom of speech and of the press is guaranteed to people unless the topic is religious, at which time such speech becomes "unconstitutional." "Hate Crime Laws" have begun to abridge our freedom of speech even more, making it politically incorrect and sometimes unlawful to say anything that might offend anyone or any group. We already have laws that should make the punishment fit the crime. Hate crime laws are for only one purpose – to take away your freedom of speech and even your thoughts.

All of this was caused by the lie that the ACLU started and that the courts have reinforced, that "there is a WALL OF SEPARATION BETWEEN RELIGION AND GOVERNMENT in the Constitution." I would like to say it loud and clear. There is NOTHING in the U.S. CONSTITUTION about a WALL OF SEPARATION between government and Christianity. There is, however, a first amendment that guarantees that "The government shall make no establishment of religion, NOR PROHIBIT THE FREE EXERCISE THEREOF." In other words, they cannot establish a state church as they had in Europe, nor can they deny us the right to practice our religion. With the elimination of prayer, Bible reading, and removing the Ten Commandments from our schools and our courts, the ACLU and the courts have helped to destroy the Christian heritage on which our country was built.

Chapter 11
WE WILL DESTROY PATRIOTISM AND THE TRUTH OF AMERICA'S HERITAGE!

"Continual and constant degradation of national leaders, national institutions, national practices, and national heroes must be systematically carried out.... By attacking the character and morals of Man himself, and by bringing about, through contamination of youth, a general degraded feeling, command of the populace is facilitated to a very marked degree."

While ignorant of our country's politics and history, students are well-acquainted with the details of movie stars and their love affairs. Destroying history and the landmarks that represent eras of history are part of the strategy that enable Communists to destroy traditions and heritage. People not knowing their background of moral standards and civic duties makes it possible for a totalitarian government to form. Learning history is a process of understanding what kind of values the nation was built on and what it takes to preserve these traditions. Only then will its people cherish what they have today and pass it to the next generation.

The Marxist Howard Zinn is the author of a history book entitled "A People's History of the United States." It revolves around the premise that all the heroic deeds and inspiring episodes from American history are shameless lies, and that the true history is all about cruelty and depravity.

History is being re-written by teachers, books, movies, television and the Internet. An economics professor at a university in Boston published an article in 2004, in which he equated the terrorists who carried out the 9/11 attacks with the American rebels who started the War for Independence.

The Library of Congress has many original books locked away from the public. Our history, written by professors and textbook publishers is lacking in depth, historical truth, and background. What is included in textbooks is so watered down that it is boring, incomplete and often incorrect.

America was discovered and settled principally by Christian people searching for freedom to worship and to spread the Gospel. Even Christopher Columbus stated,

"It was the Lord who put into my mind (I could feel His hand upon me) the fact that it would be possible to sail from here to the Indies. All who heard of my project rejected it with laughter, ridiculing me...The fact that the gospel must still be preached to so many lands in such a short time - this is what convinces me."

But, instead of this in our history books, we read only that he was a greedy adventurer desiring a way to India and its wealth and causing the death of an Indian civilization. Because our children have not been taught to think for themselves and to learn from history, they are destroying our heritage as well as our statues.

George Washington, one of the most heroic and great leaders of our country, our first president and a most devoted Christian, is relegated in our history books to a small story about a cherry tree. That may be true or untrue, who knows, but every student of history in this country should know the true story of Washington. This is one that has been removed from most history lessons.

Fifteen years after the battle on the Monongahela, part of the French and Indian War in 1775, the commander in chief of the Continental Army, George Washington, returned to the same Pennsylvania woods and sat down with a respected Indian chief who had led his warriors in that battle.

Recounting that battle, the chief said, "I called to my young men and said, 'Mark yon tall and daring warrior? He is not of the red-coat tribe—he hath an Indian's wisdom and his warriors fight as we do—himself alone exposed. Quick, let your aim be certain, and he dies.' Our rifles were leveled, rifles which but for you, knew not how to miss—'twas all in vain, a power mightier far than you shielded you."

Then he continued, "I am old and shall soon be gathered to the great council fire of my fathers in the land of the shades, but ere I go, there is something bids me speak in the voice of prophecy: Listen! The Great Spirit protects that man (pointing at Washington), and guides his destinies—he will become the chief of nations, and a people yet unborn will hail him as the founder of a mighty empire. I am come to pay homage to the man who is the particular favorite of Heaven, and who can never die in battle."

When history books are rewritten, when whole buildings are redesigned to hide these kinds of heroes, these kinds of sentiments about our nation's forefathers and their reliance upon God, then it seems that there might indeed be a conspiracy to make us forget where we came from and the brave generations before us. As we remove and demolish statues of heroes, who are still heroes, regardless of which side they were on, reducing to rubble the history of conflict and triumph, we should remember what the real aim of our enemies is.

"If we could effectively kill the national pride and patriotism of just one generation we will have won that country. Therefore, there must be continual propaganda abroad to undermine the loyalty of the citizens in general and the teenager in particular."

"By these means the patriotism of youth for their Capitalistic flag can be dulled to a point where they are no longer dangerous as soldiers. While this might require many decades to effect, Capitalism's short term view will never envision the lengths across which we can plan."

The billions of dollars spent on a government education is not only wasted, it is being used to destroy this country. Students are not being taught to read and think for themselves but instead are being taught to be ashamed of America, our heritage, and all that America stands for. Prime examples are the young black football players who refuse to stand for the National Anthem. They have had opportunities that in other lands they might never have had but they do not feel any allegiance to America. They could use their privilege and wealth to inspire the young people of their race but instead they teach them by example to hate America.

When I was in South Africa, there were always children asking me about America. I remember especially one very tiny African boy who said, "I can fit in your suitcase. Please take me to America." Wherever I go, people are studying English so that they can come to America. We should be proud of a country full of people who have worked together to do great things. There have always been evil people who do terrible things but for the most part, we have a heritage of bravery, goodness, and faith for which we can be proud.

As we come upon another tremendously important election, we should look at where our country is headed and what kind of candidates we have? People, young and old, are confused about what is best for our country. The leaders of the Democrat Party for the most part, but it includes some Republicans, are trying to take our country down a path that is against the principles on which this nation was founded. We are at a cross-roads of political ideologies and most people haven't a clue as to what or who is trying to take over the country. These ideologies include:

Socialism: "Take from the rich and give to the poor." It sounds good if you are the poor, until everyone gives up and decides "Why work? We'll just let the government take care of us." Eventually all become poor, and only the ones in power are rich. Feeding at the government trough sounds good until there is nothing left in the trough. You have had a taste of socialism during the Covid-19 experience when the governors and mayors told you to stay in your houses while they went out to boat on the lake or march in the streets.

Socialism's true believers, like Bernie Sanders, who calls himself a "democratic socialist," say they want equality and fairness, but it is a deadly lie that seems to have a special appeal to young voters who have confused "socialism" with charitable instincts, and view political correctness as necessary so that no one is offended. Some only pretend to fight for the injustices that they see in our country while really thinking that they are entitled to live for free off the government or their parents. They fight for tolerance as long as it is what they wish to tolerate.

Communism: Most people say they don't want Communism but many people are hiding the fact that they do. No matter how important or unimportant they are, there is in many people the desire to control other people. They want power over the masses. They want to be the ruling class. That is the Communist plan. "We will take over your industries, your schools, your farms, and your banking systems. Your government knows what is best for you so we will tell you what to do and where to work and everyone will get the same pay, if there is any. We, the government, will get our own healthcare, our own wealth and our own privileges, and you cannot do anything about it." It is one step away from the One World Government that they are now calling Globalism.

Globalism: The globalists have prepared a world-wide catastrophe, (a pandemic, riots, terrorism, assassinations,) so that one person working with the United Nations and secret societies, bankers, media, and technology gurus can come to the rescue and take control over every nation, dividing the world into areas, spying on everyone and everything, removing all freedom and demanding your allegiance and obedience. The difference between communism and globalism is that, although control is with the one at the top in communism, in globalism, we now have the technology to monitor what each and every person is doing or saying, sometimes even thinking.

Islam: "Kill all infidels!" is not just a slogan. Although there are many peaceful Muslims, Muslims, for the most part, are reared to believe that anyone who is not a Muslim should be killed. Contrary to what the media and some government leaders would have you believe, Islam is not a religion that wants to live peaceably side by side with its neighbors. They do not integrate, they invade. Look at their history. Look at the countries where they have taken over. Look at the way they are openly stating their hatred of America. Look at the terrorist attacks that are happening every day around the world in the name of Islam. The atrocities committed on women and children are well documented. Any woman who thinks she will be better off under a Muslim government has never been in a Muslim country for long.

Democracy: A government of the people, by the people and for the people which gives all men equality of opportunity, rights, and treatment, instead of allowing the government, bureaucracies and a chosen few to make all of the decisions. It is a free enterprise system that promotes individualism and achievement. But because it is run by majority, the majority can change the precepts by which it is governed and can enlarge the scope of the government. That can eventually lead to anarchy and to an oligarchy, (a few men in control,) or a monarchy, (one man in control.)

A Republic: A form of government in which power is explicitly vested in the people, who in turn exercise their power through elected representatives. It is a constitutionally limited government in which the power is created by a written

Constitution, which is adopted by the people and changeable by them only by its amendment, and is exercised by officials, elected by the voters, who have powers divided between three separate Branches: Executive, Legislative and Judicial. That is what America was created to be.

This anecdote about Benjamin Franklin emphasizes how fragile our democracy is: When he was asked, after the Constitutional Convention, "Well, Doctor, what have we got—a Republic or a Monarchy?" He replied, "A Republic, if you can keep it."

What does this have to do with the election? You vote according to the kind of country you want. If we do not take control of our government, our government WILL TAKE CONTROL OF US!

Chapter 12
WE WILL DESTROY YOUR ECONOMY
WITH TAXATION!

"If the American People EVER allow the banks to issue the currency, their children will wake up homeless on the continent their forefathers established."– **Thomas Jefferson**

Communist Manifesto:

"The masses must at last come to believe that only excessive taxation of the rich can relieve them of the 'burdensome leisure class' and can thus be brought to accept such a thing as income tax, a Marxist principle smoothly slid into Capitalistic framework in 1909 in the United States. This, even though the basic law of the United States forbade it and even though Communism at that time had been active only a few years in America."

I leave the majority of these quotes without explanation as I believe they speak for themselves as to the thoughts of each individual and express their ideas of what they believe.

In 1865, during the time Lincoln was attempting (and thereafter succeeded) in creating a debt-free currency for the People; **this editorial was printed in the London Times.**

"If this mischievous financial policy [of creating a debt-free currency], which has its origin in the American Republic, shall become permanent, then that government will furnish its own money without cost! It will pay off its debts and be without debt. It will have all the money necessary to carry on its commerce. It will become prosperous without precedent in the history of the world. The brains and the wealth of all countries will go to America. That government must be destroyed or it will destroy every monarchy on the globe!" **Lincoln was assassinated April 14, 1865.**

"Let me issue and control a nation's money and I care not who writes its laws." - **Mayer Amschel Rothschild**

"Whoever controls the volume of money in our country is absolute master of all industry and all commerce ... and when you realize that the entire system is very easily controlled, one way or another, by a few powerful men at the top, you will not have to be told how periods of inflation and depression originate." — **President James A. Garfield,** just a few weeks before he was assassinated on July 2nd, 1881.

In 1913, the passage of the Federal Reserve Act delegated the power of printing US currency to the large private **banking corporations.** The Federal Reserve System is the Central Banking System, created by bankers who were allowed to write their own set of rules for the banks. Congress even gave them the right to issue the nation's money. They could create money out of nothing, with 600 stockholders claiming 6% of any profits. All of our federal income tax goes to pay the interest to this banking cartel.

Rockefeller and other bankers bribed Congress to pass the Federal Reserve Act over Christmas Break in 1913. President Woodrow Wilson signed it but regretted it later. He said,

"I am a most unhappy man. I have unwittingly ruined my country. A great industrial nation is controlled by its system of credit. Our system of credit is concentrated. The growth of the nation, therefore, and **all our activities are in the hands of a few men**."—**President Woodrow Wilson**

Congressman Louis McFadden, House Committee on Banking and Currency Chairman (1920-31), stated:

"When the Federal Reserve Act was passed, the people of these United States did not perceive that a world banking system was being set up here. A super-state controlled by international bankers and industrialists...acting together to enslave the world."

Later the gold backing was removed enabling the Fed to print infinite amounts of paper money, lending to the US government at interest! (Essentially, lending the people their own money and charging them interest for it!)

"The real menace of our Republic is the invisible government which like a giant octopus sprawls its slimy legs over our cities, states and nation. At the head is a small group of banking houses... This little coterie...runs our government for their own selfish ends. It operates under cover of a self-created screen... seizes...our executive officers...legislative bodies...schools... courts...newspapers and every agency created for the public protection." — **John F. Hylan,** Mayor of New York, **1922**

"Every effort has been made by the Federal Reserve Board to conceal its power. But the truth is the Federal Reserve Board has usurped the government of the United States. It controls everything here; and it controls our foreign relations. It makes or breaks governments at will. No man, and no body of men, is more entrenched in power than the arrogant credit monopoly, which operates the Federal Reserve Board and the Federal Reserve Banks. These evildoers have robbed this country of more than enough money to pay the national debt.
—Congressman Louis T. McFadden before the House of Representatives, in the midst of the Great Depression, 1932.

A federal income tax was then instituted as a means for paying the Fed back the money that the government would require in the pursuit of building a one-world-government.

While authorizing Congress to levy taxes, the Taxing and Spending Clause of the United States Constitution permits the levying of taxes for two purposes only: to pay the debts of the United States, and to provide for the common defense and general welfare of the United States. Taken together, these purposes have traditionally been held to imply and to constitute the federal government's taxing and spending power.

But, in 1913, the Sixteenth Amendment was ratified, clear in its aim: The Congress shall have power to lay and collect taxes on income, from whatever source derived, without apportionment among the several States, and without regard to any census or enumeration!

Congress enacted an income tax in October 1913 as part of the Revenue Act of 1913, levying a 1% tax on net personal incomes above $3,000, with a 6% surtax on incomes above $500,000. With a few ups and downs, it has continued to rise and has become so complex that it requires a huge government department to manage and enforce its gargantuan reach.

"By interfering with the economics of a nation to the degree that privation and depression come about, only minor shocks will be necessary to produce, on the populace as a whole, an obedient reaction or hysteria."

A Corona Virus hysteria and an instigated protest rally, with mob violence inserted into it, is an excellent recipe for not only anarchy but economic chaos. When it happens right before an extremely pivotal election, you know it was planned.

> "In a nation under conquest, such as America…A boom is as advantageous as a depression for our ends for during prosperity our propaganda lines must only continue to point up the wealth the period is delivering to the selected few to divorce their control of the state. During a depression one must only point out that it ensued as a result of the avarice of a few and the general political incompetence of the national leaders."

The candidates that are running for president in the Democratic Party have been reading right out of the Communist playbook. Their goal is not just communism but a One World Government.

There are people in our government, in our media, in our corporations, in our justice system, and around the world who are very serious about a "One World Order, so it is imperative that they take control of the government. They have been working toward it for many years and through many presidents' terms. If you really want to understand where we are right now, you have to research which corporations, banks, universities, teachers unions, railroads, wind farms, etc. are being subsidized by the federal government and which lawmakers are being subsidized by wealthy financiers.

> "We in the Congress have a moral and constitutional obligation to protect the value of the dollar and to understand why it is so important to the economy that a central bank not be given the unbelievable power of inflating a currency at will and pretending that it knows how to fine tune an economy through this counterfeit system of money." — **Dr. Ron Paul,** Congressman, R-Tx

Chapter 13
SECRET SOCIETIES

The Order of the Illuminati

The Order of the Illuminati was founded on May 1, 1776 by Adam Weishaupt, an apostate Catholic Priest who was financed by the House of Rothschild. Weishaupt, in 1848, hired Karl Marx to write "The Communist Manifesto" to promote their Communistic beliefs. Weishaupt said at the time,

> "The great strength of our Order lies in its concealment; let it never appear in any place in its own name, but always covered by another name, and another occupation"

(John Robison, *Proofs of a Conspiracy*, 112).

Myron Fagan, mentioned previously, described with documentary evidence, how this Illuminati became the instrument of the House of Rothschild to achieve a One World Government and how every war during the past two centuries was fomented by this group. Freemasonry was to be one of the chief organs used to conceal his order in plain sight, revealing only what was necessary to keep the average person engaged but ignorant of the whole plan. (Nesta Webster, *Secret Societies and Subversive Movements*, 209-210).

Council on Foreign Relations

> "The Council on Foreign Relations (CFR) is the American Branch of a society which originated in England...(and) believes national boundaries should be obliterated and one-world rule established." — **Carroll Quigley,** from his book Tragedy and Hope, **1966**

The CFR is considered the most powerful organization of its kind because it controls many of our government officials whose job it is to form government policies. It is directed by the global banking families who regulate a very small number of banking and investment firms who control our money. They use propaganda to convince the public and Congress to support their policies. The goal of this invisible government is to transform the United States into a socialist state which would have to be more subjugated before being turned into a dictatorship and eventually to a one-world government.

"The ultimate aim of the CFR is to create a one-world socialist system, and to make the U.S. an official part of it."
Dan Smoot, a former member of the FBI Headquarters staff in Washington, D.C

"The CFR, dedicated to one-world government, financed by a number of the largest tax-exempt foundations, and wielding such power and influence over our lives in the areas of finance, business, labor, military, education, and mass communication-media, should be familiar to every American concerned with good government, and with preserving and defending the U.S. Constitution and our free-enterprise system. Yet, the nation's right-to-know machinery, the news media, usually so aggressive in exposures to inform our people, remain conspicuously silent when it comes to the CFR, its members and their activities." — Congressman John Rarick

Although one of the most powerful entities in the country, few Americans have even heard of the Council on Foreign Relations or the other secret societies such as the Bilderbergs and the Trilateral Commission.

The United Nations and the Globalist Elite have been pushing for the supremacy of international and foreign law over the Constitution and American law for decades. Some are flagrantly becoming more public as America becomes more pagan. One such society is the Bilderbergs.

The Bilderbergs
The Bilderberg group is an organization of political leaders and international financiers that meets secretly every spring to make global policy. There are about 110 regulars—Rockefellers, Rothschilds, bankers, heads of international corporations and high government officials from Europe and North America.

The Bilderbergs have three primary functions:

1. To gain power – Whether it is societal, economical, political, military, mental, or even occult, they want total control.

2. They want access to privileged information, details that can win or lose fortunes.

3. They intend to shape the understanding, worldview, and ambitions of society.

Trilateral Commission

The Trilateral Commission represents a skillful, coordinated effort to seize control and consolidate the four centers of power—**Political, Monetary, Intellectual, and Ecclesiastical**." — **Senator Barry Goldwater** from his 1964 book "No Apologies"

1993 — CFR member and Trilateralist, Henry Kissinger, writes in the Los Angeles Times concerning NAFTA:

"What Congress will have before it is not a conventional trade agreement but the architecture of a new international system...a first step toward a new world order."

Thank goodness Donald Trump saw the danger and removed us from NAFTA.

FBI/CIA

"For some time I have been disturbed by the way the CIA has been diverted from its original assignment. It has become an operational and at times a policy making arm of the government." — **President Harry Truman**

Operation Mockingbird is a good example of what Truman might have been referring to. It was a program of the United States Central Intelligence Agency (CIA) that began in the early 1950s, was created to disseminate stories that promoted the Communist cause, and received money from Moscow. Just as a communist government would, it manipulated the news to distribute its own propaganda for its own purposes. The existence of this program was denied until it was uncovered in Senate hearings in the mid-1970s. Investigations revealed illegal wiretapping, domestic surveillance, assassination plots, and human experimentation.

The human experimentation initiated by Allen Dulles, then-director of the CIA is known as MKultra, and was the CIA's mind control program. Between 1953 and the late 1960s, CIA researchers subjected thousands of U.S. and Canadian citizens without full consent of the participants, to experimental tests, including electric shock therapy, brain surgery, and LSD dosing, in order to identify methods for controlling human behavior.

The CIA also has a history of plotting political assassinations.

Perhaps that is why Susan Duclos reported that before Donald Trump even took the Oath of Office, Democratic Senate Minority Leader Chuck Schumer issued an outright threat against President-Elect Donald Trump, saying that Trump's taking on the Intelligence community was "really dumb" because "they have six ways from Sunday at getting back at you."

The CIA owned over 250 media outlets in the 1960s, spent close to a billion dollars (in today's dollars) spreading misinformation, and had people doing its bidding in every major city in the world, so it is not surprising that they were able to disseminate the idea that by calling those who questioned the clandestine activities of the government conspiracy theorists, it would discredit them. "Conspiracy theory" since then has been used to shut off debate, to signal that it is something we can't speak about because it is so ridiculous.

The CIA directed all of its bureau members to use the term as a weapon of ridicule to discount any controversial accounts of their operations. With the cooperation of media personalities, the public has completely accepted official accounts of unresolved events such as the Kennedy assassination, the Oklahoma City Murrah Federal Building bombing, 9/11, the Sandy Hook Elementary School massacre, and most recently, the George Floyd video.

"With this [CIA] memo and the CIA's influence in the media, a primary element of contemporary propaganda campaigns using the conspiracy theory/ist label is to suggest that citizens' distrust of government imperatives and activities tends toward violent action."

Tyranny is the result of not being able to be informed and to freely discuss what is happening in government, to not be able to ask questions about propositions such as Agenda 21, "Common Core," the dangers of vaccines, etc. without being ridiculed and labeled a "conspiracy theorist."

But there is a secret conspiracy that is now becoming known because the planners evidently feel that it is so close to fruition that they needn't hide it anymore. It is a scheme that is as old as man. It is being used by Satan, with the assistance of deceived people, to take over the world.

Chapter 14
UNITED NATIONS

Churchill, Roosevelt, and Stalin appointed Algier Hiss to be the first Secretary-general of the U.N. for the founding conference held in San Francisco, in 1945. (Remember he was a Soviet spy.)Every single Secretary-General since the U.N's formation has been a socialist and of the fifteen men who have been appointed to the position of Undersecretary-General of Political and Security Council Affairs, every single one of them has been a communist! These communists have three main areas of responsibility:

- Control of all military and police functions of the United Nations peacekeeping forces.

- Supervision of all disarmament moves on the part of member nations

- Control of all atomic energy ultimately entrusted to the United Nations for peaceful and "other purposes".

Agenda 21 is a sustainable development action plan drafted by the United Nations, detailing the goals by which powerful people think society should be organized. The stated goals are redistribution of population based on resources, but the unstated goals are confiscation of private property and population control.

The following list, from Truthstream Media does a good job of translating the "global goals" of the United Nations into language that we can understand.

- **Goal 1:** End poverty in all its forms everywhere.
  - **Translation:** Centralized banks, IMF, World Bank, Fed to control all finances, digital one world currency in a cashless society

- **Goal 2:** End hunger, achieve food security and improved nutrition and promote sustainable agriculture
  - **Translation:** GMO - genetically modified organism

- **Goal 3**: Ensure healthy lives and promote well-being for all at all ages

- **Translation:** Mass vaccination, Codex Alimentarius - a collection of international standards, guidelines and codes of practice for food

. **Goal 4:** Ensure inclusive and equitable quality education and promote lifelong learning opportunities for all
  - **Translation:** U.N. propaganda, brainwashing through compulsory education from cradle to grave

. **Goal 5**: Achieve gender equality and empower all women and girls
  - **Translation:** Population control through forced «Family Planning»

. **Goal 6**: Ensure availability and sustainable management of water and sanitation for all
  - **Translation:** Privatize all water sources, don›t forget to add fluoride

. **Goal 7**: Ensure access to affordable, reliable, sustainable and modern energy for all
  - **Translation**: Smart grid with smart meters on everything, peak pricing

. **Goal 8**: Promote sustained, inclusive and sustainable economic growth, full and productive employment and decent work for all
  - **Translation:** Trans Pacific Partnership, free trade zones that favor megacorporate interests

. **Goal 9**: Build resilient infrastructure, promote inclusive and sustainable industrialization and foster innovation
  - **Translation:** Toll roads, push public transit, remove free travel, environmental restrictions

. **Goal 10**: Reduce inequality within and among countries
  - **Translation:** Even more regional government bureaucracy

. **Goal 11:** Make cities and human settlements inclusive, safe, resilient and sustainable

- **Translation:** Big brother, big data, surveillance state

. **Goal 12:** Ensure sustainable consumption and production patterns
  - **Translation:** Forced austerity

. **Goal 13:** Take urgent action to combat climate change and its impacts
  - **Translation:** Cap and Trade, carbon taxes/credits, footprint taxes

. **Goal 14:** Conserve and sustainably use the oceans, seas and marine resources for sustainable development
  - **Translation:** Environmental restrictions, control all oceans including mineral rights from ocean floors

. **Goal 15:** Protect, restore and promote sustainable use of terrestrial ecosystems, sustainably manage forests, combat desertification, and halt and reverse land degradation and halt biodiversity loss
  - **Translation:** More environmental restrictions, more controlling resources and mineral rights

. **Goal 16:** Promote peaceful and inclusive societies for sustainable development, provide access to justice for all and build effective, accountable and inclusive institutions at all levels
  - **Translation:** U.N. "peacekeeping" missions, the International Court of (blind) Justice, force people together via fake refugee crises and then mediate with more «U.N. peacekeeping» when tension breaks out to gain more control over a region, remove 2nd Amendment in USA

. **Goal 17:** Strengthen the means of implementation and revitalize the global partnership for sustainable development
  - **Translation:** Remove national sovereignty world-wide, promote globalism under the "authority" and bloated Orwellian bureaucracy of the U.N.

These goals sound good and reasonable and that is the reason that you must look at the ideas behind the words and envision the results. These are not only the goals of the United Nations. They are also the goals of the secret societies who are the creators of the United Nations.

The genocides in Africa that have been promoted secretly by the United Nations makes you wonder what is going on behind closed doors. How peaceful are those U.N. "peacekeepers?"

An Associated Press (AP) investigation revealed in 2017 that more than 100 United Nations (UN) peacekeepers ran a child sex ring in Haiti over a 10-year period, luring girls and boys as young as 12 for sex with candy and cash and none were ever jailed.

The report further found that over the past 12 years there have been almost 2,000 allegations of sexual abuse and exploitation by peacekeepers and other UN personnel around the world. As early as 2004, Amnesty International reported that under-age girls were being kidnapped, tortured and forced into prostitution in Kosovo with UN and NATO personnel being the customers driving the demand for the sex slaves.

In Cambodia, Mozambique, Bosnia, and Kosovo, reporters witnessed a rapid increase in prostitution after UN and NATO peacekeeping forces moved in. Amnesty said victims were routinely raped "as a means of control and coercion"

A July 30, 2018 dossier by Andrew Macleod given to Britain's Department for International Development, claimed that in the last ten years, UN aid workers had raped over 60,000 people. The dossier estimates that the organization currently employs at least 3,300 pedophiles. According to a U.N. report, allegations of sexual abuse and exploitation in U.N peacekeeping and political missions rose significantly in 2019, with allegations against civilian personnel nearly doubling,

Chapter 13
THE MEDIA

We have all enjoyed President Trump referring to the media as the "Fake News." But it is apparent, if you investigate other sources, that the journalists and reporters are all saying the same things and that they are spouting false narratives used to promote fear, hatred, or disgust with the president. It is important to know what the aim of the media really is and the quotes below will give you an indication of how biased they really are.

"If I allowed my honest opinions to appear in one issue of my paper, before twenty-four hours my occupation would be gone. **The business of the journalists is to destroy the truth, to lie outright, to pervert, to vilify, to fawn at the feet of mammon, and to sell his country for his daily bread.** You know it and I know it, and what folly is this toasting an independent press? We are the tools and vassals of rich men behind the scenes. We are the jumping jacks, they pull the strings and we dance. Our talents, our possibilities and our lives are all the property of other men. We are intellectual prostitutes." — **New York Times editor, John Swinton,** in reply to a toast at a banquet in his honor in **1880**

"The news and truth are not the same thing." — **Walter Lippmann,** prominent American journalist, **1889-1974**

"Our job is to give people not what they want, but what WE decide they ought to have." — Richard Salant, President of CBS News

"We are grateful to the Washington Post, The New York Times, Time Magazine and other great publications whose directors have attended our meetings and respected their promises of discretion for almost forty years. It would have been impossible for us to develop our plan for the world if we had been subjected to the lights of publicity during those years. But, the world is now more sophisticated and prepared to march towards a world government. The supranational sovereignty of an intellectual elite and world bankers is surely preferable to the national auto-determination practiced in past centuries." **–David Rockefeller,** David Rockefeller, founder of the Trilateral Commission, June, 1991.

"We know in the not too distant future, a half dozen corporations are going to control the media. We took this step (merger) to ensure we were one of them" —**Time Warner spokesperson.**

"One of our best-kept secrets is the degree to which a handful of huge corporations control the flow of information in the United States. Whether it is television, radio, newspapers, magazines, books or the Internet, a few giant conglomerates are determining what we see, hear and read. And the situation is likely to become much worse as a result of radical deregulation efforts…and some horrendous court decisions. Television is the means by which most Americans get their "news." Without exception, every major network is owned by a huge conglomerate that has enormous conflicts of interest. This is an issue that Congress can no longer ignore." — **Congressman Bernie Sanders,** *The Hill* (12 June 2002)

Public sentiment is everything. With public sentiment nothing can fail. **Without it nothing can succeed. He who molds opinion is greater than he who enacts laws. — Abraham Lincoln**

Chapter 14
LIES, PLOTS AND PLAGUES

"The end of war is the control of a conquered people. If a people can be conquered in the absence of war, the end of war will have been achieved without the destruction of war. A worthy goal, and the glory of Commmunist conquest over the stupidity of the enemies of the People. The spread of Communism has never been by force of battle, but by conquest of the mind."

"The high office of the president has been used to foment a plot to destroy America's freedom, and before I leave office, I must inform the citizens of their plight." — **Pres. John F. Kennedy; 1963; ten days before he was assassinated.**

"The answer to the Kennedy assassination is with the Federal Reserve Bank. Don't underestimate that. It's wrong to blame it on [CIA official James] Angleton and the CIA per se only. This is only one finger of the same hand. The people who supply the money are above the CIA." - **wife of accused assassin Lee Harvey Oswald**

The CIA admitted in court that they were involved with the planning stages of Kennedy's assassination but the media was not about to reveal that. The media has always cooperated and colluded with elitists and CIA.

"We can't be so fixated on our desire to preserve the rights of ordinary Americans." - **Bill Clinton** USA Today—3-11-93

"Waiting periods are only a step. Registration is only a step. The prohibition of private firearms is the goal" — **Janet Reno,** Attorney General

Our task of creating a socialist America can only succeed when those who would resist us have been totally disarmed. — **Sara Brady,** Chairman of Handgun Control, to Senator Howard Metzanbaum, *The National Educator* (January, 1994)

CLEAR AND PRESENT DANGERS

Wikipedia: False flag operations are covert operations conducted by governments, corporations, or other organizations, which are designed to appear as if they are being carried out by other entities. The name is derived from the military concept of flying false colors. – False Flag Ops are often used to convince citizens that they are in "grave danger" so governments can get public support for wars against the "new supposed enemy," or to surrender their liberties.

The present "pandemic" and the George Floyd protest marches with the economic and social destruction that has attended them has not only altered our country but it has altered out expectations. As a result of the "pandemic" we have allowed our government to tell us to stay home, wear masks, and "forget your business, your life." As a result of the George Floyd anarchy, we are all told to accept destruction and chaos without any expectation of law and order and for all of us to just "Shut up!" "You have no right to object to what they are doing to our nation."

It was bad enough after 9/11. Few American's realize how many rights were lost or compromised from the Homeland Security Act, the Patriot Act. We just quietly got in line, let them scan our bodies as well as our luggage and accepted the fact that we had lost more freedom to the government. There are today surveillance devices of one variety or another in all modern TV's, computers, cell phones, land lines, some cars, and other electronic devices. Your government is listening and watching you.

> "This campaign against the American people…is systematic psychological warfare. It is orchestrated by a vast array of interests…the money center banks and multinational corporations, the media, the educational establishment, the entertainment industry, and the large tax-exempt foundations.
> **— Senator Jesse Helms**

Socialism, Communism, Islam, Banking Cartel, U.N. agendas, New World Order - all have one goal – to control all the people, all the resources, all the wealth. They want equality for everyone but themselves.

> "Those who give up their liberties for security deserve neither and will lose both." **—B. Franklin**

Chapter 15
NEW WORLD ORDER

For thousands of years, secret societies and their agents have been assassinating kings, arranging government overthrows, creating hostility and chaos to accomplish their goal of a one- world government. It is a plan developed by the financial elite of this world, orchestrated by the devil himself, to destroy the national governments of the country and to form a large centralized global government with the goal of total control **of the world.**

Karl Wojtyla, aka Pope John Paul II:

"By the end of this decade we will live under the first One World Government that has ever existed in the society of nations… a government with absolute authority to decide the basic issues of survival. One world government is inevitable."

James Warburg, son of CFR founder Paul Warburg [Banking family], before the Senate Foreign Relations Committee on Feb. 17, 1950,

"We shall have world government whether or not you like it— by conquest or consent."

The "War on Terror" and, I believe, the COVID-19 pandemic and the race riots have been manufactured by the planners of the New World Order to create more chaos. The agents of the NWO use their money, power and control to instigate these crises, so that when the people don't know where to turn, they will be there to rescue, pretending to be their saviors, when in reality they are working to make them slaves.

With their manufactured conflicts they continue to keep the world in fear and with their power and money they control politicians, the media, the stock market, and wars. They control the future of nations by manipulating their economies and stoking every fire of dissension they can enflame.

President Hosni Mubarak of Egypt, in the New York Times (April 1995)

"The renewal of the nonproliferation treaty was described as important "for the welfare of the whole world and the new world order.""

December 7, 1988 — In an address to the U.N., **Mikhail Gorbachev** calls for mutual consensus:

"World progress is only possible through a search for universal human consensus as we move forward to a new world order."

Fidel Castro, Dictator of Cuba, to the United Nations, **1979,**

"We must establish a **new world order** based on justice, on equity, and on peace." (Look how that turned out in Cuba.)

Pretending to be peaceful, these despots have financed every major war, not only for the profitability of it, but to ensure the bankruptcy of the nations and their total dependence on the NWO financiers. Countries are given away and treaties are arranged that will benefit the goal of a one-world government.

Madeleine Albright, U.S. Secretary Of State:

"Today, I say that no nation in the world need be left out of the global system we are constructing."

President George Bush in a speech to Congress on SEPTEMBER 11, 1990, said this:

"[The war in Iraq is] a rare opportunity to move toward an historic period of cooperation. Out of these troubled times…a New World Order can emerge."

Some people have seen the danger and tried to warn America. Myron Fagan was one of them. A Jewish American writer, producer and director, he launched a one-man crusade in the 1940's, against what he claimed was a "Red Conspiracy in Hollywood." (He served as Writer Director with Pathe Pictures, Inc., then owned by Joseph P. Kennedy, father of the late President Jack Kennedy.)

In 1945, Mr. Fagan attended a meeting in Washington D.C. where he was shown a set of micro-films and recordings of the SECRET meetings at Yalta attended only by Franklin Roosevelt, Alger Hess, (Remember Hess was a Russian spy,) Harry Hopkins, Stalin, (He was the Russian dictator who had killed millions of his own people,) Molotov, and Vishinsky, when they made the plan to deliver the Balkans, Eastern Europe and Berlin to Stalin. As a result, Mr. Fagan wrote two plays: Red Rainbow (in which he revealed that entire plot) and Thieves Paradise (in which he revealed how those men plotted to create the United Nations to be the "housing" for a so-called Communist, One-World Government).

The Red Conspiracy in Hollywood was set up to produce films that would aid the One World Communistic Government plot. Their plan, and it was successful, was to destroy the morals, values and religious heritage that had made America a strong nation. Fagan took a stand to reveal what they were doing. He also made a recording, in which he revealed how Jacob H. Schiff, (related to Adam Schiff?) was sent to the United States by the Rothschild's to further this Illuminati plot and to get control of both the Democratic and the Republican Parties.

Fagan told how Congress and our Presidents were seduced into giving over control of our money system and creating the Income Tax and how Schiff and his co-conspirators created the Council on Foreign Relations in order to control our elected officials, gradually enslaving them by the United Nations and a One World Government.

"It is a conspiracy – a Satanic criminal conspiracy to enslave the world and abolish families, Christianity, and Freedom. This conspiracy has been so effective because they conceal themselves and operate from the shadows and through deceptive front movements."

Myron Coureval Fagan (October, 31 1887 - May, 12 1972)

In 1968, an American journalist, Jurian Meaessen, wrote one of the first reports on the New World Order, stating that the masonry organization is behind several studies including vaccines and mass castration and sterilization. Since then, the organization has evolved and is now one of the more powerful in the world.

QUOTES CONFIRMING the NEW WORLD ORDER

1975— In Congress, 32 Senators and 92 Representatives signed A Declaration of Interdependence, written by Henry Steele Commager. The Declaration states that:

"we must join with others to bring forth a new world order... Narrow notions of national sovereignty must not be permitted to curtail that obligation."

Congressman John Danforth (R-Mo)

"I have never seen more Senators express discontent with their jobs....I think the major cause is that, **deep down in our hearts, we have been accomplices in doing something terrible and unforgiveable to our wonderful country.** Deep down in our heart, we know that we have given our children a legacy of bankruptcy. We have defrauded our country to get ourselves elected.»

Alabama Governor George Wallace, once pointed out,

"There's not a dime's worth of difference between the Democrats and Republicans."

Congresswoman Marjorie Holt refused to sign the Declaration saying:

"It calls for the surrender of our national sovereignty to international organizations. It declares that: our economy should be regulated by international authorities. It proposes that we enter a 'new world order' that would redistribute the wealth created by the American people."

David Rockefeller admitted proudly that he was part of a secret organization, called the New World Order, which has only one goal in mind: world domination. He said, in 1993,

"This present window of opportunity, during which a truly peaceful and interdependent world order might be built, will not be open for too long — we are on the verge of a global transformation. All we need is the right major crisis and the nations will accept the New World Order."

Congressman Larry P. McDonald

"The drive of the Rockefellers and their allies is to create a one-world government combining supercapitalism and

Communism under the same tent, all under their control...Do I mean conspiracy? Yes I do. I am convinced there is such a plot, international in scope, generations old in planning, and incredibly evil in intent."

McDonald was killed in the 1983 Korean Airlines **747, shot down by the Soviets.**

The majority of our Congressmen have betrayed America. Betrayals have come from both parties. In fact, the parties themselves are controlled by the super elite.

The elites have already taken control of the world's financial system. Our politicians, by legalizing a fraudulent scheme called the Federal Reserve, made it possible for private banking corporations to get control of our money supply, by printing money and charging the world for it, ensuring the debt that will enslave the nations.

The labor of the people assessed by the Income Tax, another completely unconstitutional mandate of the government, are the only resources keeping the system going. They are essentially using our own money to control the news media, politicians, stock markets and any other institution that can be bought.

George Herbert Walker Bush, September 11, 1990

"Out of these troubled times, our objective — a new world order — can emerge. Today, that new world is struggling to be born, a world quite different from the one we have known."

Dr. Henry Kissinger, Bilderberger Conference, Evian, France, 1991,

"Today, America would be outraged if U.N. troops entered Los Angeles to restore order. Tomorrow they will be grateful! This is especially true if they were told that there were an outside threat from beyond (i.e., an "extraterrestrial" invasion), whether real or promulgated, that threatened our very existence. It is then that all peoples of the world will plead to deliver them from this evil. The one thing every man fears is the unknown. When presented with this scenario, individual rights will be willingly relinquished for the guarantee of their well-being granted to them by the World Government."

As this is being written, the Globalists' strategy is being implemented right here in the USA. I wanted to go on record as being aware and trying to warn people about the evil that some cannot see, so I posted this on Facebook:

"We all know what is happening. It is exactly the Globalists' plan to take over America and the world.

1. Create a depressing atmosphere, economic depression, fear of food shortages. (The COVID-19 pandemic)

2. Instigate an inciting event, a crisis of some kind. (The heinous killing of George Floyd and the continuous display of the video)

3. Stoke civil unrest in major U.S. cities. Use the media to inflame the public. (Protests gatherings and marches)

4. Use special agents, masquerading as police, to attack the protestors. With more agents, escalate the event by having blacks attack the real policemen. Involve and arm inner city gangs, already angry and easily induced to violence in which they can vandalize and loot with impunity. (Piles of bricks in trucks and the middle of streets, money being transferred)

5. Demonize the police so that they cannot do their jobs, make it imperative to call in the National Guard. Disguise special agents as protestors and have them fire upon the Guard. The victimization of the blacks and the criminalization of the police will insure the anarchy that comes from abandoning the laws. (Instigators coming from out-of-state)

6. Meet the demands of the rioters and allow them the freedom to destroy and deface stores, monuments and statues, reinforcing the idea that riots work and that we the American citizens, will allow them to rule over us. (Governors and mayors who are afraid)

7. The Globalists' desire is to continue the riots with enough Americans killed and property destroyed in major cities, that they can bring in the U.N. "Peace Keeping"Force, which are mostly merciless mercenaries.

8. A stock market crash with the accompanying panic will be a "fait accompli" because economics control elections. Voters usually vote according to their wallet.

9. The Globalists' immediate goals will be realized when they have disarmed American citizens, suspended the Constitution of the United States and imposed martial law.

If it doesn't work this time because of Donald Trump, it will continue to be planned and carried out until it does work. Pray that God will strengthen President Trump and open the eyes of the people.

Chapter 16
THE REAL DONALD TRUMP

When Donald Trump declared that he would run for president, I thought it was absurd because of his reputation for being brash and immoral and uncaring. When one of my Christian friends said that she was going to vote for him, I was incredulous and I asked her, "Why on earth would you vote for him?" She replied, "I prayed about it."

So I started praying and ended up also voting for him. And I am so glad I did. I can't imagine anyone else who is stronger and could have overcome the obstacles that he has faced. With all of my heart I believe that he is God's man for the time and that God is giving us one more chance to get our lives right and change our society. This man and this opportunity has reminded many people of a heathen king named Cyrus, whom God raised up to deliver the people of Israel from Babylon and to restore Jerusalem. He said of Cyrus:

> "I summon you by name and bestow on you a title of honor, though you do not acknowledge me. I am the Lord, and there is no other, apart from me there is no God.
>
> I will strengthen you, though you have not acknowledged me, so that from the rising of the sun to the place of its setting, people may know there is none besides me. ..." Isaiah 44-45

What has this brash, non-political billionaire done for America in four years? Below are just a few of over a hundred of his accomplishments and he did it all with his hands tied behind his back, while being attacked by friends and enemies.

1. Trump signed the "Allow States and Victims to Fight Online Sex Trafficking Act" (FOSTA), which includes the "Stop Enabling Sex Traffickers Act" (SESTA) which both give law enforcement and victims new tools to fight sex trafficking.

2. Through Trump's Anti-Trafficking Coordination Team (ACTeam) initiative, Federal law enforcement more than doubled convictions of human traffickers and increased the number of defendants charged by 75% in ACTeam districts.

3. In 2018, the Department of Justice (DOJ) dismantled an organization that was the internet's leading source of prostitution-related advertisements. Investigations arrested 1,588 criminals associated with Human Trafficking.

4. Trump issued an Executive Order prohibiting the U.S. government from discriminating against Christians or punishing expressions of faith.

5. He created a White House VA Hotline to help veterans and principally staffed it with veterans and direct family members of veterans. VA employees are being held accountable for poor performance, with more than 4,000 VA employees removed, demoted, and suspended so far.

6. Signed VA Choice Act and VA Accountability Act, expanded VA telehealth services, walk-in-clinics, and same-day urgent primary and mental health care.

7. President Trump ordered a halt to U.S. tax money going to international organizations that fund or perform abortions.

8. Reformed Medicare program to stop hospitals from overcharging low-income seniors on their drugs—saving seniors 100's of millions of $$$ this year alone.

9. Trump signed an executive order this year that forces all healthcare providers to disclose the cost of their services so that Americans can comparison shop and know how much less providers charge insurance companies.

10. Signed Right-To-Try legislation allowing terminally ill patients to try experimental treatment that wasn't allowed before.

11. Record number of regulations eliminated that hurt small businesses.

12. Signed welfare reform requiring able-bodied adults who don't have children to work or look for work if they're on welfare.

13. Moved U.S. Embassy in Israel to Jerusalem.

14. Approved up to $12 billion in aid for farmers affected by unfair trade retaliation.

15. Trump secured billions that will fund the building of a wall at our southern border.

16. Trump directed the Education Secretary to end Common Core.

17. The poverty rate fell to a 17-year low of 11.8% under the Trump administration as a result of a jobs-rich environment.

18. The 25% lowest-paid Americans enjoyed a 4.5% income boost in November 2019, which outpaces a 2.9% gain in earnings for the country's highest-paid workers.

19. U.S. oil production recently reached all-time high so we are less dependent on oil from the Middle East.

20. Withdrew the United States from the job-killing Paris Climate Accord in 2017 and that same year the U.S. still led the world by having the largest reduction in Carbon emissions.

21. Trump signed the Save our Seas Act which funds $10 million per year to clean tons of plastic & garbage from the ocean.

22. Trump signed the 9/11 Victims Compensation Fund into law.

23. The Tax Cuts and Jobs Act signed into law by Trump doubled the maximum amount of the child tax credit available to parents and lifted the income limits so more people could claim it.

24. [Prior to the unexpected coronavirus pandemic] More than 7 million jobs created since election.

25. [Prior to the coronavirus pandemic] the stock market reached record highs.

26. [Prior to the coronavirus pandemic] Median household income hit highest level ever recorded.

27. [Prior to the coronavirus pandemic] We had the lowest unemployment rate ever recorded.

28. [Prior to the coronavirus pandemic] As a result of the Republican tax bill, small businesses will have the lowest top marginal tax rate in more than 80 year

So why is President Trump taking so much heat? Why is he the bad guy with Republicans as well as Democrats? Why does he get shot down from the media for every single thing? Why do judges rule against him most of the time? Because they are in the same game where there are no rules except the one that says, "Bring him down so we can destroy America before the citizens find out what we are doing and rise up in revolt." It is not black against white or brown against white or citizens against police. That was all a set-up. It is the power-hungry "elite" globalists, politicians, media, corporate heads and entertainers who are using all of it against "we, the people." And we have enough uneducated, unemployable youth capable of being bamboozled by the criminals who are paying to get the riots started, not to mention paying to create a virus that will shut the world down.

It is the One World Government agents working against all of us freedom-loving citizens who just want to live our lives with peace and dignity.

Don't you wonder what will happen when we all decide not to go to work, especially the policemen, firemen, nurses, doctors, and EMT's? What will happen if we all refuse to pay our taxes until the Congress goes to work and fixes the immigration system, the health-care system, stops the sex trafficking and crime syndicates, builds the wall, pays the police, nurses, and teachers as much as they pay themselves? It would take a revolt like that to overcome the campaign of propaganda waged against us.

They aim to take us down. Am I talking conspiracy? Yes! I am and it is much more sinister and deadly than you think.

Chapter 17
THE REAL WAR

Ask yourself, "What is really going on?"

For those of you who want to keep your head buried in the sand, do not read this. For the rest of you, there is not only a one-world conspiracy adjoined to a world-wide satanic cult at work but it is ramping up for the battle of the ages.

The Satanists are becoming more public about their activities. As they are being more accepted in society, they are becoming more contemptuous of religion and Christianity. The opening of the Gotthard Base Tunnel is an excellent example.

After 17-years of construction, which included extensive boring deep below the Swiss Alps, the world's longest tunnel, the Gotthard Base Tunnel officially opened in Switzerland, and its inaugural ceremony was filled with satanic rituals. Both inside and outside of the tunnel, the event featured performances that were "laced with graphic demonic symbolism" and broadcast live around the world. No one batted an eye.

If we had not been indoctrinated by the internet, television and movies, we would have been horrified at the scenes being played out there and in other places around the world recently. Famous people being caught kidnapping, trafficking and sacrificing children.

Jeffrey Epstein was a New York-based billionaire with ties to the world's ultra-wealthy and powerful. Accused of sexually abusing many underage girls, Epstein was finally caught, jailed, and supposedly committed suicide in a New York City jail by hanging himself on his bunk with a bed sheet. It was ruled a suicide. Sure it was!

Forced to register as a convicted sex offender a decade before, he was given a shortened jail time, thanks to people he knew, but recently was accused of sex trafficking and forcing young women and girls into participating in sex orgies. He had allegedly hosted many powerful men, such as former president, Bill Clinton, at Little St. James, his 70-acre private island in the Caribbean, known by locals as "pedophile island." Authorities did nothing to stop him.

In a video posted on November 1, Steve Pieczenik, a writer and former State Department informant spelled out the extent of the corruption in the US government,

> *"The Clintons have been involved in co-opting our White House, our Judiciary, our CIA, our Federal Bureau of Investigations, our Attorney General Loretta Lynch and our Director of the FBI James Comey for some time now."*

> *"We know that both of them have been a major part and participant of what is called the 'Lolita Express', which is a plane owned by Jeffrey Epstein – a wealthy multimillionaire – who flies down to the Bahamas and allows Bill Clinton and Hillary to engage in sex with minors,"* Pieczenik explains.

> *"As a result of the excellent work that the New York Police Department guys in tracking pedophiliacs, they also have a record of both Hillary and Bill and other people associated with the Clintons with regards to pedophilia."* (If the New York Police Department is working on this, is it any wonder that they have been attacked and kept busy with BLM and Antifa mobs?)

> *"Pedophiles and sex traffickers are everywhere. Many politicians trade girls like cattle,"* The FBI informant said.

As difficult as it is to think about sexual abuse of children, the ugly truth is even deeper and more horrifying and involves some of the world's most influential characters. It is a world-wide religion that has gone undetected by the majority of unsuspecting citizens.

> *"That top elite of 8,000 to 8,500* **worship Lucifer** *as their god, regard people as sheep to be used, and manipulate the media so as to conceal how the world really operates."*

Ronald Bernard, Former Illuminati and Dutch Banker

Part of the ritual of this satanic one-world religion is pedophilia, which is promoted by homosexuals and which ties in with the cannibalism it leads to. According to Mel Gibson, "Hollywood is an institutionalized pedophile ring," and it is where missing children are drawn into Satanic underground assemblies where they are sacrificed.

Gibson, producer and actor, appearing on the Graham Norton Show , spoke of the Satanists in the movie industry who "harvest the blood of children" and who "eat their flesh." According to Gibson,

"They are using and abusing kids. They churn through a huge amount of kids every year. Their spiritual beliefs, if you can call them that, direct them to harvest the energy of the kids. They feast on this stuff and they thrive on it."

The producer said, "This isn't anything new. If you do some research you will see it's a metaphysical, alchemical phenomenon and you can find it behind the scenes in all the dark eras in history. It's a dark, multidimensional occult art and practice, used by secret societies in the last few hundred years for social programming and mind control, and raised to a zenith by Hollywood in America in our era."

The secret society referred to is the Illuminati, the globalist organization which controls the media, the government and the financial powerbrokers. Their objective is to rid the world of Christianity and to imprison all nations under a communistic one-world government and religion, just as prophesied in the Bible.

Even more shocking is an expose' by Daniel Lee, which reported that the Department of Health and Human Services [HHS] were using Child Protection Services as a front to sexually exploit and traffic innocent little children by the hundreds of thousands. Daniel Lee's Attorney, Michael Dolce, who speaks from experience from representing children abused in foster care, wrote an opinion piece published by Newsweek last year (2018) stating that the nation's foster care system is set up to sexually traffic children."

The majority of children recruited into the child sex-trafficking slave trade come through foster care, where state "Child Protection" welfare agencies place children who have been removed from their homes. That information was being reported as far back as 2013. www.huffpost.com/ entry/stopping-the-foster-care...

Oct 29, 2013, "Most of the children who are being bought and sold for sex in our nation are foster care children. In the states that are tracking these children the following, devastating numbers reveal that in 2013, 60 percent of the child sex trafficking victims recovered as part of a FBI nationwide raid from over 70 cities were children from foster care or group homes. Author: Malika Saada Saar"

The CIA-Operation Mockingbird [OMB] media has a vested interest in keeping these vile acts hidden. The CIA-OMB fake journalists want to protect themselves for participating in or being allied with pedophiles (Democrats and Republicans). Whether it is Hollywood entertainers, sport stars, politicians, judges, doctors, lawyers, Wall Street bankers, Ivy League academics, virtually all of the most elite members of society are involved in this perversion of anything human, in order to be famous, wealthy and powerful.

These monsters have an imitation of the Catholic mass called the Black Mass and the victims offered in it are human beings, and often babies. An extension of the Black Mass is abortion, which is considered a sacrifice to Satan. Abortion gives the devil special power over man. And we in America have allowed more than 60 million babies to be sacrificed.

Chapter 18
THE GREAT AWAKENING

In the last several years we have heard of the 8.8 earthquake in Chile, that followed the massive earthquake in Haiti a few months before. There are many all over the world not reported. The United States thinks that only the west coast is vulnerable but that is not so. All you need to do is examine the seismography information on the internet, to realize that we are receiving shocks in the center of the U.S. also. NBC reported that the annual number of "great" earthquakes nearly tripled over the last decade.

I don't want to be an alarmist but Jesus said, "When you see earthquakes in diverse places, it is one of the signs of the times. I know that there have always been earthquakes, but I think they are getting a little too close to home with shorter intervals.

However, the shocks of earthquakes are not nearly as alarming to me as the shocks of what is happening in Washington, D.C., where our government is supposed to be governing "of the people, by the people and for the people."

The people in power manipulate the elections so that their candidate is elected and they do not care about who becomes president of America, because if they get their way, the America we know and love will not be there. It will be a division of a one-world government. We will have been forced into it by the economic chaos that they are creating and the power that they will control over every part of our system, government, banking, industry, health care, and housing. It is their plan and unless we pray and God has mercy on us again, their plan will be carried out.

So, what is the answer to being able to keep our country free, healthy and prosperous?

Government is not the answer. Ronald Reagan said,

"The most terrifying words in the English language are: I'm from the government and I'm here to help." Big government wants to control America and tax us out of existence.

Politicians are not the answer. They are stealing from the American people without any shame. Reagan also said,

"I have wondered at times about what the Ten Commandments would have looked like if Moses had run them through the U.S. Congress. "

Obama tried to give away America, selling out to the highest bidder. He and the socialists, Democrats and Republicans, believe that you can control the population if you promise to give them enough benefits. Thomas Jefferson said,

"A government big enough to give you everything you want, is strong enough to take everything you have."

Doctors are not the answer. We like to think they are but doctors' mistakes are the third leading cause of death. Most of them are caring, over-worked and doing their best but they were taught prescription medicine and their patients have been raised to accept unhealthy lifestyles that can be hidden for a while with a pill. And government paper-work is making it impossible to stay in business. And sometimes you have medical "experts" who contribute to the chaos.

Our courts are not the answer. They are filled with unjust judges who are making laws, (which is unconstitutional for that body to make,) that are destroying our country. They are ignoring the Constitution and the God who has blessed and protected us.

So, YOU are the key.

You say, "But, I am only one and I am not important."

Hitler was only one, and he killed six million Jews. Madelyn Murray O'hair was only one and she got prayer removed from our schools. Norma McCorvey was only one and her lawsuit, Roe v Wade, led to the murder of over 60 million babies. Christopher Columbus was only one and he found a new world. Harriett Beecher Stowe was only one and she influenced the start of the Civil War. Mother Teresa was only one and the whole world came to the slums of India to help her. Billy Graham was only one but he preached the Gospel all over the world. Many times an election has been won by just one vote. It has always been one, usually going against everyone else, who has made a difference.

I repeat, "You are the most important. You hold the key to saving this country. You are the answer.

"I have learned that in order to bring about change, you must not be afraid to take the first step. We will fail when we

fail to try. Each and every one of us can make a difference."
Rosa Parks

It is time for all of us to stand up as one and let our voices be heard, to take action to restore justice and freedom for now and for the future, to restore the power of government to the people where it belongs. People are waking up to see what is happening and there is a Resistance movement through-out the world that is fighting against the satanic plans for a "New World Order." The Resistance is 100% committed and dedicated to dismantling the NWO in all its forms and removing it's stranglehold on the nations and people of the world.

Please do your part to help educate your friends and family to be aware of the evil plot of the Globalists and Satanists, but also to join the resistance movement, joining in prayer for our country, while voting and making your voice heard. Make a promise to yourself and your children to always stand for truth, justice and freedom.

Educate your children. Resist the indoctrination of our children in our schools.

- Refuse to believe the media. Turn it off.

- Take part in restoring truth and justice.

- Guard your home and family.

- Be an informed voter.

- Become a prayer warrior.

Pastor Peter Muhlenberg, a Lutheran minister heard Patrick Henry's famous "Give me liberty or give me death" speech in 1775, and was inspired to enlist in the Revolutionary War. He said,

> "If you do not choose to be involved, if you do not fight to pro-tect your liberties, there will soon be no liberties to protect."

Chapter 19
THE SOLUTION

"When people ask, 'Why has the Lord done this?' It shall be answered, 'Because they forsook the Lord God of their fathers.' Our fathers have trespassed, and done that which was evil in the eyes of the Lord our God, and have forsaken him, and have turned away their faces from the habitation of the Lord, and turned their backs. Therefore the wrath of the Lord was upon them and he has delivered them to trouble, to astonishment, and to jeering, as you see with your eyes." 2 Chronicles

When the devastation of **9-11** happened to this country, my grandchildren asked, "Why did God allow that to happen?" I said, "We have turned our backs on God and for a moment He turned away from us." We want and beg for His mercy, but do we deserve His mercy when we simply accept what the media, politicians, entertainers, sports elites and corporate moguls tell us we must accept?

They tell us that we are sexist if we are against abortion, that we are bigots if we are against homosexuality, that we are sexually repressed if we are against pornography, adultery, divorce, and broken homes, and if we object to the name of Jesus being blasphemed and being ridiculed, we are hypocritical fault-finders.

We Christians have been so politically correct that we have allowed our society to be completely destroyed. Or was it because we just didn't care enough to let our voices be heard?

We didn't even object when the cross, the Ten Commandments, the Bible and prayer were taken out of our schools, our public places, our military memorials.

Do you think for one moment that God will hold us guiltless for the millions of babies killed, for the foundation that we allowed to be destroyed underneath our children, for the cruelty done to children because of pornography, alcohol, drugs, and sex trafficking, for the filth that we have allowed to spew into our homes?

We, so-called Christians, have set back and allowed it. We have spent our time working for more money and more things and being consumed by our addiction to pleasure, entertainment and sports.

That is what destroyed Sodom and Gomorrah. Not the sodomy and the homosexuality. Those were merely the last symptoms of a diseased culture which finalized the deserved judgment. What the Bible said destroyed Sodom was pride, gluttony, too much leisure and not providing for the poor.

We are guilty. It would take a miracle to save this land from judgment. Are we praying for a miracle? Are we even praying?

America was never perfect. Our forefathers were never perfect. But we had a heritage of faith in God and as long as we chose to live under God's laws, we prospered. If you travel anywhere in the world, you will come back to America and be thankful. It is so much better than anywhere else on earth. Do we really want to give up on her? Is there any chance to return to a more stable, peaceful, loving America?

When our nation was started, it was begun with Christian principles and heritage and we prospered. Nevertheless, the Supreme Court, in only twelve months in 1962 and 1963, divorced this nation's schools and public affairs from more than three centuries of its heritage. Thirty-nine million students and over two million teachers were barred from doing what had been done since our nation's founding: pray in school.

At the Constitutional Convention of 1787, the representatives from each state were deadlocked, demanding whatever was in their own states' interest. Some were leaving because it looked hopeless to come to any consensus. Then the nation's elder statesman, Benjamin Franklin, rose and quietly said,

> "I have lived, Sir, a long time, and the longer I live, the more convincing proofs I see of this truth: that God governs in the affairs of man. We have been assured, Sir, in the Sacred Writings that except the Lord build the house, they labor in vain that build it. I firmly believe this. I also believe that without His concurring aid, we shall succeed in the building no better than the builders of Babel; we shall be divided by our little, partial local interests; our projects will be confounded; and we ourselves shall become a reproach and a byword down to future ages. I therefore beg leave to move that, henceforth, prayers imploring the assistance of Heaven and its blessing

on our deliberation, be held in this assembly every morning before we proceed to business."

Believing that what he said was true, the delegates dismissed, attended church and prayed for three days. They were finally successful in the great undertaking of creating a government for America only because they stopped to pray.

George Washington also passionately believed in prayer. In his first Inaugural Address, he said,

"No people can be bound to acknowledge and adore the invisible hand which conducts the affairs of men more than the people of the Unites States. Every step by which they have advanced to the character of an independent nation seems to have been distinguished by some token of providential agency. We ought to be no less persuaded that the propitious smiles of Heaven can never be expected on a nation that disregards the eternal rules of order and right, which Heaven itself has ordained.

He warned in his Farewell Address,

"Of all the dispositions and habits which lead to political prosperity, religion and morality are indispensable supports. In vain would that man claim the tribute of Patriotism, who should labor to subvert these great pillars of human happiness. Reason and experience both forbid us to expect that national morality can prevail in exclusion of religious principle."

So we must pray. I don't mean pray as you run or drive-through prayers as you go to sleep at night, but substituting earnest prayer over our families and our country for one or two television programs every night. No, it isn't entertainment. It will take time away from your television or computer time, but if we do not want to see America and our children fall to the enemies that surround us, we'd better all get on our knees and pray and then stand up and let our voices be heard.

"For our struggle is not against flesh and blood, but against the rulers, against the authorities, against the powers of this dark world and against the spiritual forces of evil in the heavenly realms." Ephesians 6:12

No government is simply imposed on us. We get what we deserve.

I want the old America back. I want a government that is "of the people, by the people, and for the people," not one where the government is the boss and the people are its slaves. I want neighborhoods where people visit and help one another. I want families who pray together and work together and stay together, where children grow up with a mother and a father instead of complete confusion. I want schools that are educating instead of brainwashing, where children are safe and happy and learning for the joy of it. I want television that inspires us instead of destroying us mentally, emotionally and spiritually.

Was there ever an America like that? Perhaps not, perhaps it was just a dream. But I want an America where I can still dream about the possibility. I want back the dream that is America. Please, please pray for our country. Pray as if your life depended on it. Because it does.

EPILOGUE

If I had more time, I would also alert you to the MANDATORY GLOBAL VACCINATION, the GLOBAL TRACKING SYSTEM, the ELIMINATION OF OUR CURRENCY SYSTEM, the HATE CRIMES LAW which is censoring of our free speech, ARTIFICIAL INTELLIGENCE, the NATIONAL ID, HAARP, the suicide/ assassinations/plane crashes, the MUSLIM BROTHERHOOD'S CONNECTION TO THE BLACK LIVES MATTER movement, ANTIFA, and many more but this little pamphlet has grown too long already and it is urgent to get it out, so that will have to wait until another day.

Many people are talking about and are afraid that this is the end of the world but if you know your Bible, you know that after a seven-year tribulation, there will be a thousand years of peace on earth, so it is not the end of the world. However, I don't know anyone who would want to go through the tribulation to get to the Millennium.

To be honest, it is beginning to look as if we are in the tribulation period or at least quickly approaching it, and if you watch the news or see what is being shown on television and the internet, you could certainly be tempted to start hoarding food supplies and stashing weapons. Anyone who has looked at the rebelliousness around us will have to admit that we deserve judgment for the wickedness and evil that has covered America and the whole earth.

Knowing where I am going when I die takes away my fear and thus I consider this the most exciting time to be on this earth. At any moment we may see Jesus coming in the clouds to get His church.

But for those who do not know the Lord Jesus as Savior and who want a more real-world, here and now, hope, there actually is a movement to combat the sinister plot of Satan and his Globalists by a group of patriots called Q-anon who are recruiting ordinary citizens to pray and to open their eyes to see what is happening to our country and fight for freedom. President Trump is part of it and he is doing his best to keep the conspirators off-balance so that justice will be done. It is important for us to see that what the media are showing us are lies and we must not fall for them.

The enemy has infiltrated even the Q movement so that when you research, you must use discernment to understand what is truth and what are lies. But these patriots are people who have discovered the horrible dens of iniquity and the sinister schemes of the Satanists and Globalists and are trying literally to rescue the captives and save America. They are real super-heroes but must remain unidentified. Thousands around the world are joining with them. If we pray and if we vote, we have a chance to stop the annihilation of Western civilization.

There is actually some hope, based on the Bible, that we could possibly last for another hundred years or so. That is what happened to the extremely wicked people of Nineveh. When warned by Jonah to repent or prepare for God's judgment, they all repented of their sins and God withheld his judgment for a hundred and thirty years.

> "When God saw what they did and how they turned from their evil ways, he relented and did not bring on them the destruction he had threatened." (Jonah 3:10) All along, God says,

> "I take no pleasure in the death of the wicked, but rather that they turn from their ways and live."Ezekiel 33:11 According to God's Word, that is all that we need to do, repent and turn from our wicked ways and live.

Many prophets are saying that we are going to have a revival and God says,

> "If my people humble themselves and pray and seek my face and turn from their wicked ways, I will hear from heaven, forgive their sins, and heal their land." (2 Chronicles 7:14)

Wouldn't it be worth some serious prayer to see your children and grand-children receive one hundred- thirty more good years? That is a spiritual answer because, in reality, this is a spiritual problem.

But, our greatest hope is Jesus, Lord and Savior. He wants to deliver us from our enemy, cover us with the robe of righteousness and snatch us up to Heaven. What is a better hope than that? If we turn to God, accept His Son as our Savior, we can escape the tribulation period and live eternally with Him.

> "They tell how you turned to God from idols to serve the living and true God, and to wait for his Son from heaven, whom he raised from the dead—Jesus, who rescues us from the coming wrath." 1 Thessalonians 1:9

There are world-changing situations occurring right now and everything is moving so rapidly that it hardly seems logical to publish a book when the Internet is spitting out information faster than you can comprehend it. It really is just like the prophet, Daniel said,

> "…even to the time of the end: many shall run to and fro, and knowledge shall be increased."

But we should all remember the verse before it:

> "And they that are wise shall shine as the brightness of the firmament; and they that turn many to righteousness as the stars forever and ever." (Daniel 12:3,4)

I pray that this little book will make a difference.